Digging the Trenches

NORTH
SEA

HOLLAND

R. Waal
R. Maas

Zeebrugge
Ostend

Antwerp

BELGIUM

Dunkirk

Ghent

Cologne

Brussels

Aix-la-Chapelle

R. Yser
JULY 1917
JUNE 1917
Passchendaele

Ypres
Messines Menin
St.Omer Bailleul
Hazebrouck Armentieres
Lille
Lillers MAR. 1915 Neuve Chapelle
Béthune La Bassée
SEPT.-1915 Loos
St.Pol Lens
APRIL 1917 VIMY RIDGE Douai
ARTOIS Arras
APRIL 1917
Doullens
Bapaume
JULY 1916 Albert
Amiens
R.Somme JULY 1916 Péronne
St.Quentin
PICARDY Ham
Montdidier La Fère
Lassigny
Noyon Laon
Compiègne
Soissons APRIL 1917 APRIL 1917
R.Oise
R.Ourcq Reims
Senlis
Chantilly

R. Schelde

R. Lys
R. Schelde

Liège

Namur R.Meuse
Huy

Charleroi

Valenciennes
Maubeuge
R.Escaut
Cambrai
R.Sambre
Le Câteau

R.Oise
Guise

Mézières Sedan

Givet

ARDENNES

Neufchâteau

Luxembourg
Virton

Longuyon
FEB. 1916

Briey
FEB. 1916

GERMANY

R. Meuse

R. Rhine

R. Moselle

Trier

Saarburg

R. Saar

Thionville

Metz

LORRAINE

Paris

Château Thierry
Epernay
Pt. Morin
Gd. Morin
MARSHES OF ST.GOND

R. Marne
APRIL 1917

R.Aisne

CHAMPAGNE

R. Meuse

Verdun
FOREST OF ARGONNE

St. Mihiel

R. Moselle

Morhange

Châlons

R. Ornain
Bar le Duc

R. Marne

Toul

Nancy

R. Seine

R. Moselle

R. Meurthe

Charmes

Epinal

VOSGES

ALSACE

Belfort

WESTERN FRONT

▬ ● ▬ ● ▬ ● ▬   Approximate line at end of 1914
◦│◦ ◦│◦ ◦│◦ ◦│◦   Line at end of Hindenburg Retreat, February 1917
▬▬▬▬▬   Line on 11th Nov. 1918

0   50
        Miles

Digging the Trenches
The Archaeology of the Western Front

ANDREW ROBERTSHAW & DAVID KENYON

Pen & Sword
MILITARY

First published in Great Britain in 2008 by
Pen & Sword Military
an imprint of
Pen & Sword Books Ltd
47 Church Street
Barnsley
South Yorkshire
S70 2AS

ISBN 978 1 84415 671 9

Printed and bound in Thailand by
Kyodo Nation Printing Services Co., Ltd

Pen & Sword Books Ltd incorporates the Imprints of Pen & Sword Aviation, Pen &
Sword Maritime, Pen & Sword Military, Wharncliffe Local History, Pen and Sword
Select, Pen and Sword Military Classics and Leo Cooper.

For a complete list of Pen & Sword titles please contact
PEN & SWORD BOOKS LIMITED
47 Church Street, Barnsley, South Yorkshire, S70 2AS, England
E-mail: enquiries@pen-and-sword.co.uk
Website: www.pen-and-sword.co.uk

Contents

Acknowledgements

This book and the archaeology it describes were the results of the team efforts of a large number of people, and the gratitude of the authors extends to all involved.

Firstly, thanks to the archaeological team, all those, both paid and unpaid, who sweated (or froze) in the trenches at various times; in particular Luke Barber, whose work on finds was invaluable, and our documentary researchers, Alastair Fraser, Steve Roberts, Ralph Whitehead and in Germany Alexander Brunotte and Volker Hartmann. Other vital technical assistance was received from Renata Peters and Dean Sully and their students at the Conservation Laboratories of University College London. We were kept safe on site by Bill Shuttleworth of Maritime and Land EOD Ltd, and Eric McVey and Rod Scott of 11 EOD Regiment RLC. Logistical support came from Chris Carling of REME, the Royal Logistic Corps, and the Belgian Army. The work in Belgium was also conducted in close cooperation with the members of the Association for World War Archaeology (AWA), in particular Marc DeWilde and Frederik Demeyere.

The projects were funded and supported by Pauline Duffy and Elliot Halpern of YAP Films (*Finding the Fallen/Trench Detectives*), Carol Walker and the Somme Association (Thiepval), and Catrine Clay at the BBC (Serre). We were assisted in France and Belgium by Guillaume de Fonclare at the Musée Historial de la Grande Guerre, Peronne, and by the Services Regional d'Archaeologie of Nord Pas-de-Calais, M. Fosse; and Somme Picardie, M. Collart. Vital help was also provided by the Commonwealth War Graves Commission, their German counterpart the VDK, and by Parks Canada and the Canadian Department of Veterans Affairs.

Finally our thanks go to Avril Williams at Auchonvillers, without whose generosity in letting us dig up her garden, and enthusiastic support of our later projects, none of what is described in the following pages would have happened in the first place.

Introduction

A FUNERAL

In the spring of 2004 the authors had the privilege of attending a funeral. The deceased was a member of the Kings Own Lancaster Regiment, killed on 1 July 1916, the legendary first day of the battle of the Somme. In attendance were a party from the Border Regiment, the successor regiment to the Kings Own, who provided a bearer party and buglers, as well as the chaplain and the Commanding Officer, along with the UK Defence Attaché from Paris and a delegation from the French armed forces. A number of local people, including the farmer who owned the land where the man had been found, and a rather surprised battlefield tour coach party were also present. This brought the number of people at the graveside to something like a hundred. It was an enormously moving experience for everyone to see the buglers in full dress with red tunics and foreign service white pith helmets playing the Last Post and Reveille over a coffin draped in the Union flag and adorned with a khaki cap and medals. Sadly the name of the soldier will never be known.

Author Andy Robertshaw with the Chaplain of the Border Regiment at the funeral of the unknown Kings Own soldier, Serre, April 2004. (*DRK*)

He is one of ninety-one men known to be missing from his battalion on that day. In the course of the service all their names were read out by members of the bearer party, which consisted of six men drawn from all ranks of the regiment, from a newly joined private to the regimental sergeant-major. It was strange to think that the man's name was almost certainly read out over his coffin, even though we will never know which of those names was his.

For the members of the archaeological team that excavated the remains, this was a special event, both for those present at the ceremony and for those who only learned of it later. It represented the conclusion of a lengthy and laborious process, not only of excavation, but also of laboratory work and archival research which had taken over six months. Indeed the process is not yet complete: the objects associated with this man's remains offer a variety of clues that are still to be followed up, and research on these continues. Until there is a name on that headstone as well as a regiment the case will never be 'closed'. Information may well yet come to light that will lead us to the specific identity of the soldier. In a sense, however, whether we ever know his name is not all that important. What is important is that he was an individual soldier of the Great War, one person caught up in that great cataclysm, and that he has now been properly laid to rest in a Commonwealth cemetery alongside others killed that day, and possibly even with some of his comrades in arms (we will never know for sure).

'Known unto God'. The headstone of the Kings Own soldier found at Serre and buried nearby in Serre No. 2 Commonwealth cemetery. (*DRK*)

When the cemetery was revisited a few months later the turf had been replaced and the grave had started to blend in with the tidy, silent ranks of headstones. However, for the excavation team that grave will always stand out, and will be a place to visit, to pay respects, and to pause on every trip to the region. In addition to the flowers planted in front (including a miniature red rose, for Lancashire, planted by the team), two small wooden British Legion 'poppy' crosses had been placed on the grave. One of these bore a faded photograph of a young man in khaki uniform, and the other a simple note expressing love and grief for a lost relative. In the short time since the funeral not one but two families, descendants of those lost on 1 July, had adopted the grave as possibly that of their ancestor; two of the ninety-one. Whether their specific man lies there or not ultimately makes no difference: for them he does, and if he isn't their man, but some other soldier, then equally he now has a family to visit him and acknowledge his resting-place.

This is what separates the archaeology of the Great War from almost any other field of archaeological activity. Excavations of sites from all eras of the past have been carried out, from the earliest prehistory to the mills and factories of the industrial revolution, but few of them have the power to enthral, connect emotionally, and even shock, to the same extent as the remains of the Great War. And it's not only the remains of the soldiers themselves that have this power, but also almost every excavated artefact, whether it be a fragment of exploded shell, a discarded corned-beef tin, or something more personal such as a toothbrush or a piece of uniform. It is this special quality that inspired the excavations described in this book.

Unfortunately, a feature that the archaeological remains of the Great War share with sites of other periods is their vulnerability. Every year the remaining evidence of the conflict is eroded by new development, road construction and urban expansion. Deep ploughing, chemical fertilisers and other modern agricultural practices also impact upon those remains in rural areas. Each of the projects described in this book therefore contained an element of 'rescue' archaeology. Each of the sites was under threat, sometimes only indirectly from farming, but in other cases directly, for example from the proposed construction of the A19 motorway around Ypres. Any archaeological work carried out on the Western Front therefore helps to 'preserve', if only in the form of written record, a part of this diminishing archaeological resource.

Recruits for the York and Lancaster Regiment drilling in 1914. At this period uniforms were in short supply, as were up-to-date weapons. (*Imperial War Museum: HU37016*)

THE WAR IN MODERN MEMORY

The First World War, the 'Great War' as its participants termed it, was an event more or less unique in British history. Up until that time the British Isles had stood behind the 'wooden walls' of the Royal Navy and although forces had participated in almost every European conflict since the Hundred Years War, our commitment of men was always relatively small compared to our population. Waterloo was won with only around 26,000 British troops on the field, accompanied by around 49,000 Prussians and 45,000 other European allies.[1] By contrast over eight million men were enlisted from Britain and her Empire between 1914 and 1918, of whom over five million spent time in France and Belgium on the Western Front. At the time, the national population in the UK was around forty-four million. It is true that the total enlistment for the Second World War was slightly higher, at around ten million,[2] but for much of the 1939–45 period Britain was not involved in significant ground combat with the enemy. The battle of El Alamein in October 1942, for example, involved only eight Commonwealth Divisions against four German,[3] at a time when Germany had in excess of 170 divisions fighting in Russia, a figure which was to rise to 185 divisions by the middle of 1943.[4] This can be compared to the nineteen British divisions involved on the first day of the Somme battle alone in 1916. The truth is that it was only during the eleven months between D-Day and the capitulation of Berlin that Britain had significant forces committed in a major theatre during the Second World War. This comment is intended in no way to diminish the sacrifice made by soldiers in other theatres in the Second World War or in that conflict as a whole, but merely to illustrate that in numerical terms the degree of involvement in European warfare that the Western Front between 1914 and 1918 represents for the UK was both unprecedented and never repeated.

A product of these numbers is the unparalleled penetration of society that the war achieved. Prior to 1914 the army was small enough to be largely 'outside' society. As now, in the early years of the twenty-first century, citizens before the Great War frequently read in the papers of

Private Arthur Sandford, pay clerk in the 7th Battalion London Regiment (the 'Shiny Seventh'), and great-great uncle of David Kenyon. His niece Edith, who grew up in his family, has her arm on his shoulder; she would become the author's grandmother. (*DRK*)

the exploits of their armed forces in otherwise little understood dusty corners of the world, and took pride in their achievements, but very few were related to, or even knew, a soldier individually. The Great War changed all that. One in five of the male population of Great Britain was mobilised into the nation's armed forces, with similar substantial contributions from the Empire and Dominions. Those of the authors' generations, born in the 1950s and 1960s, each have two grandfathers and four great-grandfathers, plus uncles and other relatives. Thus for more or less every person of British descent living in the UK today there is a better than even chance that they had an ancestor in uniform in the war (whether they realise it or not), and of those five out of eight would have served on the Western Front.

This close connection that every family in the UK has to the war is increasingly reflected in the interest in the subject. The growth of family history research, assisted by the many internet resources now available, has led to an enormous growth in the number of private researchers studying the conflict. In 1988 the war became part of the National Curriculum in history (and literature, examining the poetry) for schoolchildren, and thus classes are now learning as a matter of course about the trenches, and are visiting the relevant battle sites. This in turn feeds back into popular genealogy as children are encouraged to research family members caught up in the conflict or the names on their school or local war memorials.

It is ironic that much of this intense interest has developed only as the war is fading from living memory. Many families have been inspired to take an interest in the war experience of their relatives only after those concerned have died. The authors have heard many stories of people coming across papers or medals when clearing out the homes of relatives after death, and discovering a world of experience that was never spoken of while their relative was alive. It is a sad aspect of the experiences of many soldiers that they chose not to share with their families what had happened to them, and this silence was respected, drawing a veil over the whole subject for many years. Only now is that veil starting to lift, albeit after the key witnesses have departed.

Thus coaches bring ever-increasing numbers of people to the battlefields of France and Flanders each year. For many this takes the form of a personal pilgrimage to follow the footsteps of family members, or more poignantly to visit the graves of men they never knew, or know only as faces in old photographs. For many visitors these journeys are made in an effort to 'see the ground' or somehow share the

Tyne Cot Cemetery, near Ypres in Belgium. Some 11,952 men are buried here, making it the largest of all the Commonwealth cemeteries. Of these, about 70 per cent are unidentified, their headstones bearing the words 'Known unto God'. The names of a further 35,000 'Missing' men are recorded on the walls at the rear of the cemetery. (*DRK*)

extraordinary experience that their ancestors had, but on the Western Front this is very difficult. Getting there is very easy: a host of tour companies will take you on guided tours of varying depth, and the key areas are over-supplied with guidebooks and visitor facilities. However, it is important to think more closely about what these visitors actually see. Each of the principal battlefields is adorned with a range of monuments large and small: the largest include the Memorial to the Missing at Thiepval on the Somme, the Menin Gate in Ypres and the Canadian Memorial at Vimy. There are also the cemeteries, dotted across the landscape, each beautifully maintained by the Commonwealth War Graves Commission, and ranging in size from the intimate, with just a few headstones, to the almost unbearably large, such as Serre No. 2 or Tyne Cot.

Visiting any of these is undoubtedly a powerful and haunting experience, seeing the long lists of names on the memorials to the missing, the names and ages on individual headstones, and the rows of dead simply 'Known unto God'. The gravestones are made more poignant by the personal inscriptions. These inscriptions cost 3 pence a letter after the Great War, a powerful incitement to brevity among the poorer bereaved, while after the Second World War the public were entitled to 60 letters at a total cost of 7 shillings and 6 pence (equivalent to more than a week's wages for a private soldier). It was reported that some families were unable to pay even that amount. In practice, the Commission carried out the work regardless of payment. (The Canadian government wanted to pay for all the personal inscriptions to its fallen, while the New Zealand government felt personal inscriptions went against the principle of equality of treatment and so banned them completely! In the end the payment became voluntary and was then scrapped altogether.) Unfortunately a tour of such sites tends to impart to the visitor not a greater understanding of the experience of those actually participating in the war, but rather a fog of overwhelming grief, which while powerful is not especially enlightening. Indeed, those searching for the experience of one person, relative or not, can find themselves lost in a sea of names, an ocean of loss in which all statistics become so large that people are prepared to believe almost anything about the war as long as it is expressed in unimaginably large numbers.

THE ARCHAEOLOGICAL EXPERIENCE

For many it is sufficient merely to have experienced this passing sense of grief, to have wondered at the depth of sacrifice and the futility of it all. For others, however, a Portland stone headstone or a white marble monument is not sufficient. It tells us nothing of the misery of living in a frowsty dug-out, being shelled, or standing sentry on a freezing night, or equally of the joy of a sunny afternoon off behind the line, or a joke shared among friends who have come safely through an attack together. It is for these people that this book is intended, and indeed the whole pursuit of Great War archaeology has as its goal an effort to reach past the simple memorialisation of the war and try to present the experience of it.

This experience is two-fold. First, battlefield archaeology has the power to illuminate the experience of the soldiers themselves. Through excavation we can tell the story of their lives with a surprising degree of intimacy. Archaeology as a whole (in contrast to history, which is often the story of kings and queens, of countries and empires) almost invariably tells the story of everyday life, of the experience of ordinary people only occasionally caught up in great events. Great War archaeology is no exception: trench excavation will rarely give you much insight into the minds of the Kaiser and Haig, but it will reveal the everyday life of their troops in extraordinary detail.

The second level of experience is that of a visitor to an excavated site. We are offered the 'Experience' of the past all too often nowadays as a form of heritage marketing, but in the case of an excavated trench at least, the sensation of walking in the footsteps of Great War soldiers, in some cases even on the same trench-boards, is undeniably moving. The faceless mass of names on the memorials dissolves into a sense of the individual experience of each man, and individual excavated objects, however mundane, create frozen moments in time which can be literally held in one's hands. For the young in particular this can be especially powerful. Describing the week-long bombardment that preceded the opening of the Somme battle to a school group is met with some indifference until a few jagged shell fragments are circulated, at which point an unusual hush tends to descend.

However, it is not the sole purpose of battlefield archaeology to provide some form of 'theme park' for visitors. Those of us excavating the Great War have suffered complaints from our peers in more conventional strands of archaeology that academically the excavation of battlefields has nothing to tell us. In archaeological terms the war is very recent, and is well documented with eye-witness accounts, photographs, maps and even movie film footage, thus surely we completely understand it? On the contrary, as we hope this book will make clear, a wealth of new knowledge about the war can be gained by digging.

A most basic example of this is the assumption, made by those wishing to dismiss Great War archaeology, of the 'pulverised battlefield'. It is claimed by many (who have not looked) that there is no point in excavating those parts of the battlefield where the most significant fighting took place, as repeated shelling would have rendered the whole area a muddy soup in which archaeologically coherent features such as trenches, dug-outs or even casualties would simply not survive. Such digging was therefore pointless. The team was to learn very quickly, however, that while parts of the battlefield had suffered very heavily from shelling, such areas nevertheless retained identifiable trench lines and other constructions, and in fact the very dynamic character of the activity in these places made the archaeology most rewarding, albeit at times highly complex. Unpicking the history of even a small part of this complex battlefield thus produced a fascinating account not only of the destructive power of artillery, but also of the resilience and resourcefulness of those subjected to it.

Such work also tested the expertise and technical knowledge of the archaeologists concerned. It is another common misconception (discussed in a later chapter) that trench lines were simply created in 1914, occupied for a few years and abandoned. In fact their evolution was constant and their layout and structure changed on a daily basis. This gives archaeologists an opportunity to deal with 'sites' whose character changed not over centuries or decades, as is often the case when dealing with earlier periods of history, but over days or even hours. This is combined with a large volume of supporting documentary data which frequently records the exact time and place of events. This allows the archaeologist to test his field interpretation of events against written evidence in a way which is not possible in other periods. Frequently, what might have been considered a reasonable assumption based on excavated evidence on a prehistoric site was challenged on a Great War site by documentary sources, forcing the excavators to reconsider their normal archaeological judgement. Equally, sometimes the documents help to reinforce the archaeological conclusions. It is rare for an archaeologist to be able to identify the date of deposition of a soil layer not just to a year, but to a minute, as was the case with chalk upcast from a mine detonated at Serre. Excavation of the Great War thus has much to teach us, not only about its own history but also about the practice of archaeology itself.

THE BIRTH OF 'TRENCH TEAM' AND *NO-MAN'S-LAND*

Books about military history in their introductions typically address, if briefly, the causes and development of the particular conflict that forms their subject. In this case it is necessary to look not at the shots fired in Sarajevo which started the war, but at how the archaeology got started: where did *No-Man's-Land* come from? Who are they? The book is laid out thematically and will make reference to a series of archaeological projects, and thus it is useful to provide a brief synopsis of our work to date and to put the various sites in context.

Many visitors to the Somme will be familiar with Avril Williams' guest-house in Auchonvillers. In the summer of 1997 a small group of battlefield visitors stopped there for one night's bed and breakfast. The party consisted of archivist and historian Alastair Fraser, archaeologist Jon Price, and Andy Robertshaw (co-author of this book) then working at the National Army Museum in London. The visit was part of a weekend trip to see the principal sites on the Somme and the party had already been to Thiepval, Beaumont Hamel and Serre before arriving in time for a drink and dinner.

Next morning Avril took time to show the three an area behind her house where a group of enthusiastic Great War re-enactors had dug a hole in an attempt to prove that a now blocked hole in the cellar had once been linked to a trench. The excavation with shovels, pickaxes and entrenching tools had revealed a variety of both French and British Great War artefacts, including fired and unfired ammunition, buttons and fittings from clothing and parts of various gas masks. Some of these items had been left behind, not a few of them on the windowsill, while other less corroded items were handed to Avril who kept them in her living room. Despite the profusion and variety of objects it was clear that the unmethodical 'dig' had resulted in a great deal of damage to the site. Some items had been broken, and with no record keeping it was clear that no one would ever understand the process by which the artefacts came to be where they were found. There was no formal catalogue of what had been found and no security, and some of the more 'interesting' artefacts had already been taken as souvenirs. Others were to be stolen over the next few months, some after illegal metal-detecting in the garden by guests.

After a brief discussion it was decided that the only way to protect and record the site was to conduct a systematic excavation of the trench at least as far as the property boundaries. As a result a small team returned to Auchonvillers in the autumn and conducted a weekend excavation employing straightforward archaeological techniques. The results were

Excavation work in Avril Williams' garden at Auchonvillers. The recently excavated section of trench in the foreground links with the restored and sandbagged section leading to the cellar of the house. (*DRK*)

good and documentary research carried out by Alastair Fraser helped to build a better picture of what was discovered. The following spring a larger team of what had become nicknamed 'Trench Team' spent a hectic Easter at the site, extending the excavation away from the dug-out and following the sinuous route of the trench across the garden. One surprising feature was that the base of the trench was brick-paved. A number of visitors to the site suggested that this was done when the family who owned the house returned to the site at the end of the war and began living in the cellar. In fact Alastair was able to prove that the bricklaying was the work of 1/2nd Battalion the Monmouthshire Regiment, part of the 29th Division, in the summer of 1915.

This was an early demonstration that even the most modest of excavations of a Great War site threw up surprising discoveries, and that theories about what was discovered through archaeology had to be tested against other evidence from documentary sources. At the same time artefacts frequently shed light on the events and activities in the village during the war. Work was to continue in Avril's garden each Easter until 2004, by which time the far boundary of her property had been reached, and a new home had to be found for the chickens and other livestock left homeless by the advance of archaeological progress. During these years 'Trench Team' evolved to draw in a wider group of archaeologists and Great War experts of all kinds, bonded together by a mutual fascination for the subject and a willingness (often shared somewhat bemusedly by their families) to spend holidays getting muddy in exchange only for the excitement of the archaeology and Avril's generous hospitality.

THE PROJECTS – TV JOINS IN

The work of the team expanded out of Auchonvillers in the autumn of 2003 when we were invited to assist with a BBC television project examining the German positions in the so-called 'Heidenkopf', an area of trenches that was occupied by Wilfred Owen's battalion in January 1917, in the period before the German withdrawal from the Somme battlefield. (History records that the battle of the Somme ended in November 1916, but that did not stop the fighting.) Owen's experiences there provided the inspiration for some of his poetry. As is typical of archaeological projects, the results of the excavation led not to Wilfred Owen nor indeed to 1917, but to the fighting of 1915 in the same area, and the discovery of several casualties from that fighting. The full story

Archaeologist Jon Price records a piece to camera while excavation continues on site at Bixschoote, near Ypres, during the making of the 'Finding the Fallen' television series. (DRK)

of these men is explored in the final chapter of this book, but it was significant in that it represented the team's first encounter with battlefield casualties and the archaeological challenges that follow on from such discoveries. Some of the results of these excavations were broadcast in 2004 in the BBC's *Ancestors* series.

Funding from television was also instrumental in further excavations carried out in 2005. Five projects were carried out in that year, two in Belgium, two on the Somme and one at Loos in Artois. These formed the basis of a series entitled *Finding the Fallen*, which was broadcast originally on the Discovery channel and subsequently re-edited and re-titled as *Trench Detectives* and shown on Channel 5 in the UK. While the inspiration for these excavations was to create material for television, all none the less had clearly defined archaeological objectives and were carried out to the highest archaeological standards. As was discussed earlier, sites were chosen which in several cases were under threat from development or were suffering continuing erosion from agriculture. Funding was made available by the television company to provide for the analysis of artefacts, and for the full writing-up and publication of each excavation. It has always been a guiding principle of the team's work that archaeological 'best practice' should at all times be applied on Great War excavations, and indeed this is what separates our work from much of the well-intentioned but ultimately quite amateur work which has been carried out in the past.

This was necessary not least because the laws governing archaeological excavations of any kind in France and Belgium are strictly enforced, and the team was obliged to comply with all relevant local regulations. Arguably, the protection afforded to the Western Front in France under normal legal controls on archaeology and metal-detecting is stronger than it would be for an equivalent site in the UK, contrary to the popular opinion in the UK that the French do not care about these sites. Inevitably the results of these excavations were much more interesting and complex than could ever be portrayed in a one-hour television programme, and it is hoped that this book can bring some of the additional detail of these sites to the reader. For those with a thirst for more precise facts and figures, it is the intention that the technical

Members of the Royal Irish Regiment performing a service of remembrance with the archaeological team after their participation in the first season of excavation at Thiepval Wood in 2004. (*DRK*)

reports from these, and indeed all the team's excavations, will be freely available via the internet in due course.

For those wishing to examine the team's efforts at first-hand, the excavated trench at Auchonvillers remains open for visitors by prior appointment. In addition the team has also been involved in work at Thiepval Wood. The wood was acquired in 2004 by the Somme Association, a charitable group based at the Somme Heritage Centre in Northern Ireland, which is also responsible for the management of the nearby Ulster Tower and works more generally to commemorate the involvement of Irish soldiers in the Great War. Soon after the Somme Association purchased the wood, an archaeological project was developed in cooperation with the Association to examine the surviving trenches within the wood. This work culminated in a series of sections of excavated trenches being formally opened to visitors on 1 July 2006, the 90th anniversary of the opening of the battle of the Somme and of the 36th Ulster Division's famous attack out of the wood.

The Thiepval project contrasts with the other television projects in that it is much broader in scope. The excavations for each television programme were extremely focused and limited in both area and time. After a week of excavation each site was backfilled and returned to agriculture. At Thiepval, however, it has been possible not only to keep open the excavated portions of trench but also to restore them to their original condition by replacing sandbags, revetting, trench-boards and other features. This serves to give visitors a vivid impression of what these trenches looked like originally, but also provides an on-going 'laboratory' for the team. The first job was to determine from original sources and photographs how the trenches were constructed, and to compare this with the excavated evidence. The next step was to attempt to put these details back. It rapidly became apparent that even something as apparently simple as sandbagging is in fact a dark art, only learned by sometimes painful and always physical labour. Over time it will also be possible to examine how these features survive the seasons, and how often remedial work has to be done on the trenches, even without the interference of enemy artillery.

The Thiepval Wood excavations have also benefited from the involvement of volunteers from Northern Ireland, who were not archaeologists but were able to bring not only their knowledge of the history of the site, but also their enthusiasm and the direct connection of their communities (and indeed in some cases their families) to the project. It is a feature of all archaeological sites that they sit within modern communities, and their excavation has the potential to interact with those communities. But it is not just a matter of the archaeologists teaching those communities about their past; very often local people can provide information influencing how the archaeologists understand the site. This was particularly the case at Thiepval, and has extended also to the involvement of the Royal Irish Regiment (the successor of many of the regiments that served in the wood), whose members have participated in the project. The sound of Ulster accents as soldiers from Belfast dug trenches within the wood was heard first in 1916 and repeated in 2005 and 2006, providing a striking metaphor for the historical and continuing community importance of the site. Added poignancy was lent to this work through the fact that the 2nd Battalion RIR was itself facing disbandment, and was thus about to become part of 'history' in its own right.

Chapter 1

The Trenches Today

AFTER THE WAR

By the end of 1918 the war on the Western Front had created a huge 400-mile-long scar across France and Belgium. Vast areas had been dug over and torn up by shelling. Numerous villages and several larger towns such as Ypres had been almost entirely destroyed. For some, including those in the victorious governments, the scale of the damage and the task of reconstruction seemed inconceivably large. It was even suggested in some quarters that the 'Zone Rouge' or Red Zone, the belt of most complete destruction, was beyond repair and should be left as a permanent memorial to the struggle. Similarly there was a proposal that the town of Ypres itself should be left in ruins in a similar fashion. This view of course took no account of the opinion of the people who actually owned the land. Some of the local population had hung on grimly throughout the war, others had been evacuated. Often this was carried

Destroyed buildings near Mametz, Somme. By the standards of the Western Front these buildings have survived pretty well; many were completely obliterated by shell-fire. *(Imperial War Museum: Q4181)*

out forcibly by the armies, as the locals were understandably reluctant to leave all they had in the world in exchange for the dubious security of evacuation. More or less as soon as the fighting was over many of these people hurried to return to see what remained of their homes and livelihoods. In the Somme area many evacuees returned after the fighting had moved eastwards in 1917, only to be caught up again in the German March offensive of 1918.

The result of this was a steady but largely informal and un-organised reclamation of the battlefields. Armed in some cases only with hoes and their bare hands families cleared the debris of war from their fields. Many were obliged to live in makeshift shelters, or in the bunkers and dug-outs left by the troops, while they rebuilt their homes. Most had a good idea of the extent of their property and land boundaries were soon re-established on pre-war lines. Indeed, many buildings were rebuilt using the original footings and to the same plan as those destroyed. A close look at many houses in the battle zone today reveals a join in the brickwork about 1–2 feet (0.5 metres) above the ground where the walls have been rebuilt.

Simultaneously with these unofficial efforts, the soldiers themselves were employed in clearing up. By 1917 the British and French armies had brought large numbers of labourers to France, notably from China and India, and these Pioneer and Labour battalions were put to work filling

A typical camp for the Chinese Labour Corps in Belgium, photographed probably in 1918. Similar camps were still occupied by the Corps until 1920. (*ASR*)

in trenches and repairing roads. The otherwise idle hands of fighting troops waiting to be demobilised were put to the same task. German prisoners of war also did this work as early reparations. In the case of the Chinese Labour Corps, a contract for 96,000 labourers for three years was agreed when the Emperor of China declared war on Imperial Germany, and began in 1917. As a result this Corps continued to work well after most British troops had gone home and the POWs had been released. Their death rate, as a result of flu and the dangers of battlefield clearance, was equivalent to the average dead for the British army as a whole: about 9 per cent. They had their own cemeteries, principally at Noyelles sur Mer.

The result of this process was that much of the evidence of the fighting rapidly disappeared, and only in areas of woodland or in fields too steep to cultivate did trench systems survive to any great extent. The rest were hidden below newly ploughed soil and crops. Other remains from the war took on new uses. Most obviously, the concrete bunkers around Ypres became cow-byres, but elsewhere houses were reconstructed using timbers or even iron girders from dug-outs, and fence lines were re-established using angle iron from trench revetments or even sawn lengths of light railway track. Much of this material is still in use today, and is identifiable by the trained eye. Most obvious are the corkscrew-shaped 'silent pickets' often still used for their original purpose of supporting barbed wire.

Some of this reconstruction was funded by charity. Organisations such as the 'League of Help' were set up in the UK to twin towns in Britain with destroyed villages in France and Belgium, and various collections were made to help the villagers struggling to rebuild their lives. Sometimes this was useful, in the form of donations of agricultural equipment or seed, while in other places collections were made of second-hand clothes. The appropriateness or otherwise of these garments to French peasants was not always fully considered and some of the donations must have been viewed with a wry smile by the recipients. The chief source of income for the returning refugees, however, after their own agriculture, was tourism (then as now). As soon as the Armistice was signed visitors began to flock to the battlefields in large numbers. Organised tours and guidebooks were available as early as 1919. Many of those visiting were of course pilgrims visiting the graves of the dead, but many more were simply sightseers. A souvenir market rapidly developed and the locals set about selling war memorabilia as well as refreshments. This has led to an entire class of archaeological objects known loosely as 'Trench Art'. During the war it was not unknown for soldiers to create artistic or souvenir objects out of military equipment, engraving shell-cases, making lighters out of cartridge cases and so on. A number of such objects were also made by prisoners of war. A large proportion of these objects, however, were created after the war for the tourist market by the local population who had easy access to the raw materials and a ready market. These objects now adorn the mantelpieces of many homes around the world, but they do not fall within the particular remit of this study as they do not reflect the conflict itself, but rather represent a particular response to it.[5]

As a result of all these activities most of the remaining traces of the war had disappeared from sight within a few years of the end of the conflict. The villages and towns had been rebuilt in pre-war style (albeit the new Cloth Hall in Ypres was not finally completed until 1967), and the fields returned to agriculture. The masses of military debris had been collected, and recycled or sold to tourists. In terms of its direct physical legacy, the war had vanished.

MEMORIALISATION

However, while the physical traces of the fighting were being erased, they were being replaced by a post-war memorial landscape. Cemeteries were adorned and consolidated and memorials were constructed to serve the emotional needs of the increasing numbers of visitors. The visible landscape that confronts visitors today consists principally of these cemeteries and memorials which appear all across, and in some cases dominate, the landscape. These must be given brief consideration as they shape the experience of many visitors to the battlefields, and serve to structure, or even dictate, the pattern of visitation. It should be borne in mind, however, that while such memorials can be regarded as 'archaeology' within its loose modern definition, in that they are the physical remains of the past, they do not represent the archaeology of the conflict itself, but rather a response to the conflict by post-war societies.

The most prevalent memorials on the battlefields are the cemeteries. At the most basic level these have a connection with the fighting in that they contain the dead, but their significance to visitors, and their role in the experience and understanding of the war, is more complex. In many ways the cemeteries with their ordered rows of headstones and their immaculate planting are the antithesis of what actually took place in the bloody chaos of battle. If ever death was 'dulce et decorum' it is in a

Commonwealth cemetery. This was an understandable reaction by the bereaved, as represented by the designers of the cemeteries, who were desperate to restore order and give 'meaning' to their loss. However, it takes the visitor a long way from the actual experience of battle.

The location of the cemeteries in the landscape can also be a trap for the unwary. It is easy to assume that the dead in each plot are those killed in the immediate vicinity, collected into a convenient spot. This was by no means always the case. Some cemeteries (for example Knightsbridge cemetery at Beaumont Hamel) started out as burial grounds adjacent to dressing stations. Wounded men who died in the dressing station were simply buried in a convenient adjacent field. Later, once these cemeteries had become established, other remains were brought there and added, both during the war and after. In other cases men buried in impromptu graves during the fighting, or scattered in small groups across the landscape, might be consolidated after the war into a larger cemetery. When the Thiepval memorial was constructed in the 1920s a number of small cemeteries in the surrounding fields were dug up and moved, so as not to distract people from the memorial itself. Thus many of the men beneath the headstones might have been buried and reburied on more

A chaplain places chalk blocks around a grave in a newly constructed cemetery near Carnoy on the Somme in 1916. This shows the level of care soldiers gave to their comrades' burial-places even in war time. (*Imperial War Museum: Q4004*)

than one occasion. Local people were encouraged to hand in any Allied dead they uncovered during their own clear-up operations by the payment of a bounty in cash for each soldier found. Perhaps understandably, given the mood of the times, but unfortunately when viewed through modern eyes, this system did not extend to German remains. The potential for slipping a few rags of khaki on to a corpse in place of field grey in order to claim the cash is obvious.

A by-product of this process is that we typically only see the dead of one side. The fate of the German dead was a great deal more uncertain, and while German cemeteries such as that at Fricourt do exist, they are not on the typical tourist trail. While special arrangements were being made to secure the future of the Allied cemeteries, returning refugees and those who had resented enemy occupation were clearing away the cemeteries established by the Germans, and dumping or destroying the bodies. Of the nearly 11,000 German soldiers in the cemetery at Fricourt on the Somme, more than 6,000 are in mass grave-pits, their remains having been cleared out of other scattered cemeteries in the area and reinterred all together with little regard for individual identity. At Miraumont local tradition has it that the men buried in the no longer extant

The German cemetery at Bray-sur-Somme. The text on the side of the memorial lists the names of the men in the mass-grave below; they were probably dug up from individual graves elsewhere and re-interred here en masse. (*DRK*)

German cemetery were dug up after the war and burnt in a local quarry. The cemeteries therefore tell a complicated, and highly partial, story.

The Memorial to the Missing at Thiepval also embodies another aspect of the memorialisation process. Enormous numbers of visitors pass under the arches of this memorial every year. No self-respecting tour guide would leave it off their schedule. The memorial itself, however, does not offer these visitors any real idea of the nature of the war. It was not fought over, or built by soldiers. In fact its placement in the centre of one of the most fiercely contested parts of the battlefield obscures rather than assists interpretation of that battlefield. Nor was it placed in that location in order to celebrate the victory in that area in particular. The original plan was to place it astride the road at the entrance to St Quentin, but that idea was quashed by the French government. An alternative position astride the road at Pozieres was suggested and turned down, and the crest of Thiepval ridge was only adopted as a 'third choice' option. The monument thus has little real connection with the ground on which it stands. Its design and intention have very little to do with its landscape setting, and while it dominates the Somme battlefields it does not interact with or interpret that landscape in any meaningful way. This memorial has recently been enhanced by the addition of a visitors' centre and toilets. However, this has had the slightly bizarre effect that visitors take time to look around the albeit magnificently presented centre, use the toilets, and then, confronted with limited time and a steep concrete ramp up to the memorial itself, get back on their coaches without ever visiting the monument! The authors

The Thiepval Memorial seen from the Pozieres road. It dominates the landscape, but has little direct connection to the events on that spot. (*DRK*)

have both been personal witness to this phenomenon.

Other memorials do have a tighter geographical focus. Many villages contain memorials to the divisions, regiments or Dominion contingents involved in their capture. The process of commissioning and constructing these memorials has been essentially random, dependent on the fundraising abilities and enthusiasm of the groups concerned, thus some quite small events are marked by large memorials while other substantial feats of arms pass unnoticed. Also the repeated ebb and flow of the battle across the same ground means that some areas famous for an action in one part of the war are obscured by memorials to another. The 'sunken lane' at Beaumont Hamel, scene of the destruction of the Lancashire Fusiliers on 1 July 1916, is dominated by the memorial to the exploits of the 51st (Highland) Division from November of that year, an event less well-known, and arguably less well-linked geographically, to that spot. Sadly in recent times the process of memorial building has also been corrupted by the value of the tourist Euro. The mayors and café-owners of otherwise unvisited villages are quick to see the economic potential of a new statue in their commune, quite apart from the historical merits of the particular memorialisation. The process of more formal memorialisation is also on-going. Australia is very active in erecting new memorials and refurbishing the old, and New Zealand gained a tomb to its unknown soldier as recently as November 2003.

The result of this is that it is quite difficult for a visitor to see the wood for the trees. Most visits to the Great War battlefields are essentially a tour of monuments and cemeteries, usually in order of their spectacular-ness (and the convenience of cafés and toilets). Any real explanation of the battles and their landscapes is limited to what can be seen from the foot of each monument or over the wall of the cemetery, irrespective of the fact that the field of battle might be far better understood from a point of view elsewhere. It would be a brave tour-guide who ignored all the marble and Portland stone and unloaded his coach's passengers on to an unmarked spot at the side of the road in order to explain the true military landscape under their feet.

Some sites ostensibly offer an experience of the 'real' battlefield. Two significant examples of this are the Canadian memorials at Beaumont Hamel and Vimy Ridge. It is by no means the authors' intention to denigrate the importance of these sites as locations for remembrance and national mourning, but the question has to be asked how closely the character of the war at those locations is actually represented by the preserved trench systems and grassed-over shell holes. The motivation

Excavations in progress at Beaumont Hamel, the muddy excavation site contrasting with the grassed-over neatness of the Newfoundland Memorial beyond the fence. (*DRK*)

for the preservation here reflected the suggestion that the whole front, or at least the Red Zone, should be preserved. A part of the battlefield would be kept unchanged to show the visitor what was experienced there. While this was an admirable notion in the 1920s, time was inevitably against it because the battlefield features were by nature temporary and the ravages of the weather would rapidly take their toll. Visitors in any numbers also rapidly eroded the traverses of the trenches and rounded off the earthworks. The managers of the sites were therefore forced into a compromise, somehow retaining the 'lumps and bumps', but at the same time allowing safe visitor access. The result is a tidy, if irregular, landscape of mown or grazed grass, with concrete steps in areas of heavy traffic. So long as such a site serves only as a memorial this is entirely appropriate, but sadly many visitors come to these sites hoping for (or persuaded by their guides that they will get) a sense of what the trenches were 'really like'. Unfortunately the tidy green slopes of these sites today give only a very faint impression of their character during the conflict itself.

A further difficulty with both Canadian sites, as with the Thiepval Memorial, is the planting of trees. Vimy Ridge is now heavily wooded, and the Newfoundland Memorial was deliberately planted around with trees of suitable Canadian species. The result of this is that the military topography has been dramatically altered, lines of sight have disappeared and thus the task of the battlefield guide explaining events at these locations has been rendered much more difficult. 'If you can imagine beyond those trees . . .' has become a well-worn phrase.

A site which had little to do with memorialisation but a good deal to do with the tourist Euro was the trench system formerly open at Hill 62 near Ypres. Here the character of the battlefield had been deliberately maintained by a lack of cultivation of turf and the retention of a variety of trench features such as corrugated iron, pickets and areas of wire. Given the apparent lack of maintenance and the heavy and unrestricted access granted to the public, it quickly becomes apparent to the thinking visitor that the 'trenches' on view cannot have survived over eighty years of this punishing treatment. They must have been reworked in the off-season on many occasions, otherwise the site would have been literally levelled by tramping feet. The relationship between what is visible on the site now and what was there in 1918 is thus tenuous to say the least.

Thus the visitor is left with a choice between grass and concrete, or a more convincing-looking, but essentially fake, patch of mud. This section has not been intended as a criticism of the work of the Commonwealth War Graves Commission, or Parks Canada, or any of the other organisations involved in the maintenance of the memorials on the Western Front, nor does it seek to devalue the importance of memorialisation. The point has been to draw a distinction between on the one hand how the war is remembered, how the bereaved felt (and continue to feel) about their loss, and the war's importance in the national myth of participant states, and on the other hand the character of the conflict itself and the material remains (the archaeology) of that struggle. Visitors and their guides should always try to remember that the memorials are not the same as the war itself, only a response to it. It is through archaeology that groups like *No-Man's-Land* and others have sought to get closer to the real character of the conflict.

A window on the thinking of some visitors was provided when the team was digging near the Newfoundland Memorial at Beaumont Hamel. A schoolteacher stopped his coach full of children on the road and came over to see what we were up to. He was shown sections of trench and freshly dug artefacts, and was offered the opportunity to bring his party over to see some Great War archaeology actually in progress. He declined, on the grounds that 'It would only confuse the children.' The past, it seems, needs to be tidied up a bit before it is suitable for young minds.

WHAT IS GREAT WAR ARCHAEOLOGY?

This argument that the war is not well represented by what there is to see above ground raises the question of why archaeology claims to give you any better view. It is the contention of this book that the nature of the Great War made it archaeologically a special case. All battles leave physical traces. Sometimes these can be very slight. During the Great War, however, the unprecedented degree to which troops 'dug-in' and lived their lives essentially below ground level, and stayed for long periods in one spot, means that their archaeological traces are much more substantial and widespread than those of other conflicts. The months of digging which took place on the Somme between 1914 and 1917 (and again in 1918) contrast markedly with the single day of fighting at Waterloo a hundred years earlier. Thus the Great War offers a remarkable opportunity for the battlefield archaeologist. The Western Front is in effect a 400-mile-long 'site', even if this fact is not readily apparent.

In the light of this great potential for archaeological discovery, what is it that we are actually looking for, and how do we go about it? Archaeologists broadly divide the things they find into two categories. In the popular imagination archaeology is the search for 'finds': objects or artefacts from the past. Sadly, the significance of these objects is frequently only understood by the public in terms of their rarity or monetary value. The question most frequently asked of an archaeologist in the pub is 'What's the best thing you've ever found?' Usually 'best' really means 'most rare and valuable', so the answer 'a hill-fort' often leads to confusion! In reality archaeologists are hunting for information which will allow them to better understand or imagine the particular bit of the past they are investigating. Thus the importance in terms of information may often be inversely proportional to the 'spectacular-ness' of the object. A grotty bit of prehistoric potsherd in a particular place may be extremely exciting for what it tells us about the date of a site.

This brings us to the second category, collectively known as 'features'. The word feature is simply a neutral term used to describe the particular place where objects might be uncovered. Typical archaeological features include ditches, post-holes, pits, and floor layers, or for the Great War trenches, shell craters, dug-outs and the like. Crucial to successful

A typical First World War feature, in this case a section of shallow trench at Vimy Ridge. The chalky fill is clearly distinguishable from the clay through which the trench was originally dug. (*DRK*)

archaeology is the idea of 'context', a term that describes the location and surroundings of objects. Typically a feature such as a pit might contain a range of finds – objects such as potsherds or coins, for example, thus providing their context. The clever bit is the analysis of the relationship, using the objects to tell us about the feature, such as its date and its function, and in turn the feature can inform the significance of the objects. How did they get there? Were they placed there deliberately or accidentally?

It is quickly apparent from this that for the archaeologist an object is only half the story. Where it came from is at least as important, hence the meticulous planning and recording that take place on excavations. A find with no context is essentially valueless in archaeological terms. In the case of the archaeology of the Great War this issue becomes even more important. In Roman archaeology, for example, the artefacts themselves are often studied separately from the sites on which they were found. An expert in wine jars might look at many examples from different locations and produce useful new ideas about how they were made or used. Other objects have intrinsic artistic or decorative merit: jewellery, statues and the like. With Great War objects this is rarely the case. Most objects uncovered are not new to the archaeologist. Most are rusty examples of items of equipment of which numerous examples exist in better condition in museums or elsewhere. Also, as they were mass-produced, the study of large groups of them (known to archaeologists as assemblages) is relatively unrewarding. For example, no one wishing to study the evolution and design of the .303 Lee Enfield rifle would start from excavated finds, since to do so would be relatively pointless in the face of the number of better unburied examples available to look at (both the authors have non-rusty examples in their cupboards at home).

What then is the point of digging all this stuff up? The answer lies in the context. By looking closely at where these objects were found and their relationships with one another, real insights can be gained into how life was lived in the trenches and what conditions were like. Once this information has been extracted, the objects rarely have any value in themselves, as a rusty corned-beef tin is hardly a valuable collectable. It is true, however, that some of these objects gain an emotional significance owing to the extreme circumstances in which they were used. A corned-beef tin emptied by a soldier on the Somme will always have more emotional and historical interest than one found on the local tip, but this again is about context. Unfortunately this archaeological approach has sometimes been misunderstood. It is typical practice in the team's projects for only rare and important objects to be retained after excavation. The vast majority of the material found in any one feature often consists of food tins and shell fragments. Careful record of the numbers and types of these objects is made, but the value of retaining all this rust is low and storage would rapidly become a problem. Thus after processing and cataloguing such material is often discarded. After one of our excavations, a visitor to the Somme posted a highly suspicious report of our activities on an internet newsgroup. This included a photograph of a pile of discarded shell fragments heaped in the corner of the field, the obvious implication being that discarding this material reflected an uncaring or unprofessional approach to our work. This of course was not the case, but it shows how battlefield archaeology is open to misinterpretation.

Discussion of the contextual importance of objects from the war leads to the question of fieldwalking and metal-detecting. It is common practice for visitors to the battlefield to look around and pick up a rusty

Finds expert Luke Barber recording the head-stamp from a rifle cartridge found at Thiepval Wood. Detailed recording of this kind of information helps to build up the overall archaeological picture. (*DRK*)

piece of shell fragment or a shrapnel ball to take home as a souvenir. As discussed above, the emotional power of these objects is significant. Nor would it be right for the authors to denigrate this practice too sternly, as both our homes contain objects acquired in this way. However, from a strictly archaeological perspective the practice is unfortunate. Each of these individual bits of rust has context within the enormous archaeological site that is the Western Front. Each time an artefact is removed, that site loses one tiny piece of information. Mostly this is not a problem since there's plenty of 'rust' to go around, but over time large numbers of visitors to an area will clear it of large numbers of objects. As these heavily visited locations are often those of significant events in the war, the archaeological potential of these areas can be threatened if too much material is removed without proper record.

Metal-detecting in France is illegal without a special government licence. However, a good deal goes on surreptitiously, and on a scale which is quite different from the casual visitor taking home some shrapnel. Organised groups detect at night, specifically targeting artefact-rich areas. Here the potential for real archaeological damage is very high. Of particular concern is the detection and collection of easily saleable, non-ferrous (non-iron, i.e. copper and brass) items such as buttons and cap-badges. Unfortunately these are most often found in association with human remains. Unethical detectorists will happily strip a soldier's remains of his badges and buttons for the few pounds they will make on the internet, irrespective of the fact that by so doing they have removed any chance that in the future that soldier might be identified and properly reburied with a named headstone. All of our group excavations are now protected by 24-hour security while the work is in progress. This lesson was learned the hard way when one site, which included a number of sets of human remains, was thoroughly looted. In another case only the presence of a burly member of the excavation team who was sleeping in the site-hut overnight discouraged a pair of foraging Belgians. A third, most shocking example occurred at Thiepval Wood. While we were making arrangements to start work in the wood, the custodian of the Ulster Tower handed a bin bag to the authors. In it were the bones of a soldier which had been found scattered around a hole dug by a metal-detectorist in the wood. In his haste to recover saleable objects, the looter had simply thrown the bones aside, regardless of clues to the identity of the body. The remains were passed on to the CWGC and given proper burial as an unknown soldier, but only after his previous resting-place had been thoroughly desecrated and his identity destroyed.

Thus not only is there a large amount of material out there, but each piece is imbued by context with an archaeological value that is potentially much greater than would be apparent by examining the object itself. All that rust is indeed gold in archaeological terms. This great resource of information is being gradually eroded by casual collection, criminal looting and by the simple ravages of time, agriculture and development. It is the job of the battlefield archaeologist to examine a tiny portion of this wealth of material in as much detail as possible, in order to offer a deeper understanding of these objects, and thus the lives of those whose legacy they represent.

PRESERVATION – TAPHONOMY

Any discussion of 'preserved' trenches in either memorials or commercial visitor attractions leads naturally to the question of what preserved actually means in Great War terms. This question is vital to archaeology, as the archaeologist can by definition only uncover those physical aspects of the past that have been preserved. Essentially what the archaeologist is looking for is a range of features – trenches and the like – surviving in a condition as close as possible to that when they were in use. Within that he or she is looking for objects still remaining in the locations where they were used or discarded, and in as good condition ('state of preservation') as possible. The way of finding the best sites for this kind of preservation is somewhat counter-intuitive. Conversations concerning the Western Front often come around to the discussion of where 'well-preserved trenches' can be seen. This is typically in woodland or otherwise uncultivated areas, where trench-lines and other features survive as eroded depressions in the ground which can be followed around their various traverses and junctions. A site of exactly this kind forms the focus of the on-going project at Thiepval Wood.

However, for the archaeologist such a trench is not always the best choice. While the location of such a trench is easily identifiable, that is about the only archaeological advantage. The fact that the trench has remained open to the elements means that any objects within it will have been exposed to significant environmental decay, and the trench itself will also have been eroded by wind and rain so much of its original shape

Team members examine collapsed dug-outs, visible as earthworks in Thiepval Wood. Wooded areas all along the Western Front contain such 'preserved' surface evidence. (*DRK*)

will have been lost. It is also inevitable that many interesting objects formerly in the trench will have been collected by visitors over the years. In addition, useful items such as angle iron pickets, corrugated iron and timber will have been salvaged by local farmers for use elsewhere. Thus it may be a trench, but it will be an eroded, denuded and picked-over one.

By contrast the same trench where it emerged from the woods into the farmer's field may well have been backfilled very shortly after the war. Thus not only will many of the objects within the trench at the time have remained, but also many objects that were originally adjacent to the trench may also have gone in, typically when the upcast soil forming the parapet and parados of the trench were shovelled back in. Revetting materials and other trench architecture, unless salvaged immediately at the time of backfilling, will also have been buried and protected. Trenches of this kind are essentially invisible to the untrained eye. However, they are recoverable. Some show up as soil or crop marks when conditions are right, or they can be detected by geophysical survey methods. Alternatively their locations can be established by careful surveying based on contemporary trench-maps or aerial photographs. Once uncovered, these trenches often prove to be in very good condition archaeologically. Post-war ploughing of the fields typically destroys the topmost foot or more (0.3–0.5 metres) of these trenches but below that conditions are often strikingly good.

Obviously 'well preserved' and 'clearly visible' are not the same thing. A good example of this was the project carried out at Beaumont Hamel. The team dug literally 'over the fence' from the Newfoundland Memorial site, in an adjacent arable field. Trenches could be seen within the memorial area, surviving as turf-covered earthworks, but at the fence forming the boundary of the memorial site they simply disappeared under the ploughsoil. However, as soon as that ploughsoil was removed the trenches were revealed in an extremely good state of preservation: revetting mesh and trench-boards were still *in situ*, telephone cables were strung along the sides of the trenches, and ordnance and other artefacts were scattered everywhere. After our investigation was complete the site was backfilled and has since been recultivated, once more entirely obscuring (but not destroying) those trenches. The excavation also proved an acid test for the trench layout inside the memorial park. Substantial phases of 'restoration' of the trenches here were carried out in the 1920s and again in the 1960s, and much of the record of this work has been lost. The only way to be certain that what is seen in the

An excavated trench at Beaumont Hamel, complete with trench-boards, revetting mesh and telephone cables. Prior to excavation this trench was invisible below a flat cultivated field. The level band of ploughsoil is visible at the far end of the excavation. (*DRK*)

memorial today is 'original' to the war would be to dig it. However, the external excavation proved the link between the otherwise invisible original system of trenches externally, and the visible but possibly dubious system of trenches within.

The next question concerns the condition of the objects themselves within and around these trenches. This is the 'taphonomy' referred to in the title of this section. Taphonomy is concerned with how archaeological sites come to be formed, and the processes by which objects decay over time. This is a product not only of what the object is made of, but also of its surroundings, whether buried or exposed to the air, wet or dry, and so on. In addition, when several different objects are in close proximity or a single object is made of a number of different materials, these materials can also interact to influence the preservation or decay of one another. Archaeological reports typically catalogue artefacts by material, thus a site report might include sections on ceramics, metalwork, bone items and other material types. Although common, this is a bit of a misrepresentation. When you move house you don't label boxes 'Metal items', 'wooden things' and 'plastic stuff'. Much more commonly people categorise objects by their use: 'kitchen utensils', 'office equipment', and so on. Many objects are also made of a variety of materials attached together, such as bone handles on cutlery, for example.

The reason for this digression into old-fashioned archaeology is to make the point that often it is the variability of the state of preservation of objects which allows their categorisation in the traditional way. On a site where all wood, cloth and paper has decayed away, objects might well be catalogued as 'iron' since only the iron parts have survived.

Objects which are subject to rapid decay or degradation will not be found, or will only be found in exceptional circumstances, while more robust items will come to dominate the range of objects uncovered (the 'assemblage', as defined earlier). The Stone Age is so called not only because people at that time used large numbers of stone tools, but also incidentally because these stone objects are just about all that typically survives from the period. Stone dominates the assemblage. The trick is not to take this distorted collection of objects at face value. It is important mentally to put back all the bits which do not survive in order to see the complete picture. The same is true of the Great War. The vast majority of objects that visitors to the Western Front come into contact with are made of iron, and are extremely rusty. Next most common are copper-alloy fuses, which corrode a good deal less and are thus 'better preserved'.

It is possible to visit museums of this 'rust and dust', often the collections of local farmers and other interested enthusiasts. These often contain only items of this sort, recovered from the surface of the fields surrounding each museum. The impression created by these displays is at best partial, and at worst highly misleading. A macabre sense of decay hangs over these collections, which some visitors find well suits the mood of the experience they wish to have. On the other hand a soldier

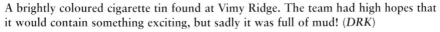

A brightly coloured cigarette tin found at Vimy Ridge. The team had high hopes that it would contain something exciting, but sadly it was full of mud! (*DRK*)

of the Great War himself would probably have as much difficulty recognising some of these objects as modern visitors, because in 1914–1918 these things simply didn't look like that. Artillery shells, for example, were always painted in a variety of bright colours to indicate their type and function. Food tins were decorated with elaborate labels, and weapons were bright and well-oiled. Thus not only is our perception of the war through photography coloured, or rather un-coloured, by the prevalence of monochrome images of the battlefields, but the artefacts themselves are also robbed of their original appearance. Pictures are all black-and-white, objects are all brown or orange. Careful archaeological excavation, as revealed in the pages of this book, has shown that the battlefields have much more to offer than rusted iron. Almost all types of objects have been uncovered during excavation, and it is through the colour and diversity of these objects that the excavations bring the trenches to life, and the true importance of digging these sites is expressed.

The survival of almost all archaeological objects is conditional on the presence of a few basic environmental factors, principally air (oxygen), water and bacteria of various kinds. Chemical reactions within and between materials also play a part. Thus even before excavations had begun across the Western Front various assumptions were made and opinions offered by our sceptical archaeological colleagues. The first of these was that Belgium would be better than France, as the low-lying, waterlogged clay soils around Ypres would typically be considered good for archaeological preservation. The damp but anaerobic (airless) conditions provided by the local clay would be expected to keep organic materials (wood, leather, cloth and so on) in good condition, and also help to inhibit rust on metal items. Stories abounded of rifles which 'could have been fired' by their discoverers, and other such pristine finds. Indeed, this proved to be the case. The excavations around Ypres have revealed objects such as leather boots, fabric in the form of groundsheets and greatcoats, and even newspapers and a wine bottle cork.

Timber features such as trench-boards and A-frame revetting (explained in a later chapter) were also uncovered in good condition. Unfortunately such preservation can be a double-edged sword. Often an object which has survived very well in an extremely waterlogged state will decay very rapidly if removed from its protective bath, sometimes almost before your eyes. It is therefore necessary to bring in quite elaborate scientific conservation methods to stabilise these items, and to store and transport them very carefully. Objects which have survived in

A wine bottle cork found at Forward Cottage, near Ypres. This item was almost perfectly preserved, down to the printing on the sides, and even the mark of the corkscrew. (*DRK*)

a drier environment are often more robust and easier to store and handle.

A pleasant surprise for the team was the good state of preservation of many artefacts recovered from the Somme in France. Here it was predicted that the drier chalky conditions would leave little more than rusted metal, and that fabric and wood would not survive. This proved not to be the case, as our first set of *in situ* trench-boards confirmed when revealed at Serre in 2003. Almost as wide a range of objects has now been found on the Somme as in the Ypres Salient, a fact that highlights the weakness of such generalisations and again demonstrates the worth of actually doing some digging and finding out rather than listening to too much negative opinion.

What the Somme sites (as well as those further north) proved is that preservation of objects is also highly variable and can depend on the smallest of details in the environment surrounding the object, often changing markedly across a single object as local conditions changed. Prime examples of this are buttons. The majority of soldiers' uniform buttons were made of brass or other copper alloys. As is well known, these corrode by acquiring a layer of green verdigris over their surface. What is significant about this is that verdigris is highly toxic, not only to us but also to bacteria. In archaeological terms this means that where materials which might otherwise be consumed by bacterial decay were next to brass objects, this decay did not take place. It was noted on several sites, particularly the excavations of the various sets of human remains at Loos and Serre, that uniforms typically survived best as ragged areas of cloth surrounding buttons. Thus lapel, coat tails and shoulder epaulettes were often preserved where the body of the garment had rotted. This was helped by the fact that these areas were also reinforced with additional folds of cloth. This was particularly advantageous to the archaeology as these areas (shoulder tabs, for example) were often the areas of the uniform which contained important regimental information, thus assisting with the identification of the individuals concerned. Perhaps rather more macabre, but no less important in this preservation process, was the human body itself. In some cases it was found that a three-way interaction was taking place not only between the button and the cloth, but also with the fats of the underlying tissue, these too assisting in the preservation of the fabric. This was effective in preservation to such an extent that in one case at Serre the original vivid red colour of an area of tunic piping was well preserved at the wrist, where not only was a button sewn on but the cloth was in close contact with the skin of the casualty.

Sometimes the results of these interactions are not obvious to the archaeologist and present a challenge to interpret them correctly. Such was the case at Beaumont Hamel. The team visited this site essentially to explore the story of 1 July 1916 and the battle of the Somme, but inevitably the excavation yielded artefacts of all periods from 1914 to 1918. Among them were large numbers of French Lebel rifle rounds, both unfired rounds and spent cartridge cases. These were deposited on the site during the original fighting and the establishment of trenches in the area by the French in 1914–15, before the British took over the sector. Such a discovery was not unexpected. What was curious, however, was the number of unfired rounds found surrounded by a small 'nest' of what appeared to be straw. Surely no one would go to the trouble of packing rifle rounds individually in straw? First, it would be unnecessary, and secondly hopelessly time-consuming. What was going on? After some thought it was realised that far from being individually packed, these were rounds that had been dropped into the relatively lush grass covering the site during this early period. Subsequently the dumping of spoil from trench excavation and earth thrown up by shell bursts had covered over these rounds along with the grass in which they lay. Elsewhere the buried grass had simply rotted away, but around each brass case corrosion products had preserved the grass for a few inches in

The Somme battlefield in June 1916. The flourishing vegetation around the British trenches is already starting to show contrast with the bare trees on the German side, stripped by the bombardment. (*Imperial War Museum: Q114*)

each direction, creating the apparent 'envelope' of straw encountered on excavation.

Not only was this a reminder that archaeological answers are not always obvious, but it also highlighted the fact that Great War battlefields were not in every case the wilderness of mud of the popular imagination. The battlefield of the early years had been grassed over. Indeed, it is one of the misconceptions about the battle of the Somme that it all took place among mud and craters. When the fighting began in July the British lines, and the no-man's-land in front of them, were largely undamaged and the first troops attacked through knee-high grass and wild flowers. Only later, as the battle dragged on into the autumn, were these fields replaced by a muddy wilderness.

In contrast to the survival of these quite delicate materials, other apparently robust items decay surprisingly rapidly. One common example is the corrosion of aluminium- and zinc-based objects. These metals are in fact highly reactive and when buried will degrade very quickly. Often they were used in the construction of artillery shell fuses, thus it is not uncommon to find a nice well-preserved brass fuse, but as often the excavator will uncover an area of what simply looks like crumbly blueish sugar, the corrosion product of a decayed aluminium fuse. Sometimes, when the two metals were used in the same mechanism, some parts survive in almost perfect condition while others have crumbled away. Incidentally, an important consideration for the archaeologist is the fact that a fuse which has decayed entirely is unlikely to function when disturbed. On the other hand an intact brass nose-cone has the potential to retain its explosive component and timer mechanism. These can be triggered and, even when detached from the body of the shell, may burst with fatal results. This is a consideration often neglected by visitors who buy shiny, polished nose-caps as souvenirs to take home, little imagining that what they have in their hands remains explosive and potentially lethal.

Sometimes the differential corrosion of materials can create quite weird effects. The Lewis gun was one of the most effective and widely used weapons of the war. It was distributed to British and Dominion platoons in huge numbers, and was eagerly adopted when captured by the Germans who never produced an equivalent weapon. The drum magazine for the gun takes the form of a one-sided circular pan, not unlike a flan-case, with forty-seven .303 rounds arranged around it with their noses towards the centre. In the centre is an alloy mechanism which both attaches the pan to the weapon and feeds the rounds into the breech. On excavation, these items come out looking not unlike a metal birthday cake. The central mechanism corrodes into a large blueish

Lewis gun drums excavated in Thiepval Wood. The corroded central mechanism is clearly visible, with displaced bullet heads poking out around it in a ring. (*DRK*)

lump, but as the corrosion products are bigger than the original mechanism the whole lump swells up over time, forcing the bullets out of the ends of the cartridges and leaving them sticking up like a circle of copper-coated candles. This is a very odd effect until you examine the processes at work, the taphonomy, in detail.

DEPOSITION – STRATIGRAPHY

The survival of objects in the ground is also of value to archaeologists in terms of their context. Once again it is necessary to introduce some terminology from traditional archaeology to explain what we mean. The process by which objects, or indeed layers of soil or other materials, end up in the ground in known as deposition. This may come about when someone dumps their rubbish, or digs a hole in one place and deposits the dug earth in another. The result is a deposit. This can be as small as a handful of charcoal from a cooking fire, or as large as the layer of ash covering several square miles which resulted when Boudicca burned Roman London. Put simply (and this means *very* simply!), the oldest deposits are buried in turn by later deposits, creating a sequence of layers, each younger than the one below it. This basic principle, that newer stuff is generally thrown on top of older stuff, is known as stratigraphy, and is one of the worldwide underpinnings of the discipline of archaeology.

Inevitably, the stratigraphy of Great War sites is a good deal more complex than this, and throws up a number of interpretive challenges. This can be explained by contrasting a section of trench with, for example, an Iron Age village. In the Iron Age people lived (generally) above ground. They dug into the ground to create ditches as boundaries and defences, and pits for storage and rubbish disposal. Thus the 'occupation' – the activities of the people – took place on the surface, and their waste was either deliberately thrown or washed by rain into the pits and ditches. On the Western Front, on the other hand, the soldiers generally lived in the pits and ditches (the trenches), and threw all their waste out on to the ground surface. Thus the normal stratigraphic picture is reversed. It is further complicated by the fact that often when the land was reclaimed after the war much of the material lying about on the surface was thrown or shovelled back into the trenches to fill them in. As a result sometimes the things thrown out last might get thrown back in first, with earlier stuff thrown in on top, reversing the normal stratigraphic 'oldest at the bottom' rule. Equally the whole lot might be

Luke Barber recording the complex sequence of deposits in a trench at Thiepval Wood. This trench was originally constructed in 1915 and reoccupied in 1918. (*DRK*)

hopelessly mixed up. The result of this is that the sequence of deposits, and the objects within each deposit, have to be considered very carefully to separate their true origins from the extent to which they have been redeposited, i.e. moved around more than once from their original position.

This process can be visualised with an imaginary but typical section of trench. When the trench is first constructed a slot is dug and the spoil piled on either side to create a parapet and parados. The sides are revetted and trench-boards laid along the floor. The garrison soldiers are a tidy lot and the trench is regularly cleaned out and maintained. As a result of this few archaeological deposits have a chance to form. Only a few small objects, probably fired and unfired rounds, are dropped and fall through the slats of the trench-boards. (Incidentally it may seem odd that so much unfired ammunition was apparently discarded, but in fact resupply was mostly freely available, and a round dropped into the mud and contaminated with traces of dirt might well cause the gun to jam at a critical moment. Given that this might well be a possible matter of life and death, it was better to simply get a fresh round out of the box.) Later, as winter comes, a layer of mud develops in the bottom of the trench, and a few more items are lost into it. Rather than dig out the old trench-board, a new one is laid on top of the mud, sealing our next archaeological deposit. This process may be repeated a number of times. In due course the 'big push' arrives and the trench is abandoned as the army advances.

Left open to the elements the trench starts to gradually weather and collapse, and a layer of clean rain-washed silt forms over the occupation deposits in the bottom of the trench. Finally, in 1918 the Labour Corps (raised in 1917), Royal Engineers, Pioneer Battalions or ordinary infantry units arrive and shovel the remaining upcast parapet material back into the trench. In so doing they shovel in all the refuse thrown out of the trench during its earlier occupation. In addition, however, they might throw in anything else which happens to be lying around. Alternatively it might be the farmer who fills in the trench, possibly using it as a rubbish dump for a number of years before it is completely full. Thus the majority of the material in the trench is not exactly *in situ*. The only material that was in there when the trench was actually in use is in the lowest deposits among the trench-boards. With luck much of the redeposited material (the stuff shovelled back in) probably originated with the troops in the trench before it was discarded, but this cannot be guaranteed, and while it may have started out in the trench it is almost inevitably *not* in its original position.

An example of this sequence at work was the trench excavated at Auchonvillers. Here the upper fills of the trench were a mass of random backfill items. Some of these were military, for example the fifty-seven rolls of unused barbed wire found heaped in one part of the trench. Others were clearly civilian rubbish, including the broken axle assembly from a farm cart. This material was probably deposited when the trenches were no longer required, indicating a period late in the war or just after it finished. The evidence here pointed to the work being done by the army as no self-respecting farmer would waste perfectly good barbed wire in such a way. But why had barbed wire been used for such a simple task as in-filling a trench when the village would, after the shelling it had suffered, have provided tons of handy rubble? Further excavation provided the answer. Beneath the rolls of barbed wire, sitting on the earthen trench floor, was a German 77mm gas shell. This was live, and as dangerous in the early twenty-first century as it had been at the end of the Great War. Perhaps a British clearing party was told to get rid of this lethal item and, in order to ensure that no one else ever made the mistake of digging it up, covered the site with barbed wire as a warning and deterrent. In this case the team had an early lesson in the potential hazards of working on a Great War site, but also gained a sense of the sheer depositional variety created in every small area of the front. This was not something that documentary evidence alone would ever truly reveal.

Lower down, material relevant to the actual occupation of the trench was found. In particular a sump was uncovered that had been cut into the floor of the trench for drainage. Such sumps have been found to contain rich deposits for archaeologists as they rapidly filled with mud and water and objects lost into them were unlikely to be fetched out again. In this case the artefacts recovered from the sump included a watch and a harmonica, both quite important personal items which if dropped on to the normal trench floor would doubtless have been retrieved. One other interesting item that was found was a single white marble tile, perhaps part of the pre-war kitchen or dairy. This was nearly over-cleaned, but careful washing revealed the words 'In Case of Fire Only' written in pencil on the polished surface. Fire was always a problem in dug-outs and precautions were rigorously enforced. Was this evidence of the nearby cellar having been provided with a fire bucket containing water or sand? The bucket had long since gone back to 'stores' or into the hands of a French family desperate for utensils, but the sign had remained. Once again, questions were raised. Who wrote the message? Did he survive? Was the sign on a bucket, and if so where in the cellar was it?

The exception to this complicated depositional process is when a trench or other feature was backfilled suddenly while it was still in use. This is not a common phenomenon in normal archaeology, the only well-known example being the eruption of the volcano Mount Vesuvius which engulfed the Roman city of Pompeii in AD 79. That site is world-famous because this event resulted in an instantaneous 'time capsule', with the lives of the inhabitants captured in full swing, in contrast to the gradual change and decay which archaeological sites usually exhibit. (In fact modern research has showed that the smothering of Pompeii by ash was a much slower process than hitherto thought, but that does not detract from its value as an example.)

Fortunately for the Great War archaeologist the prevalence of explosions on the Western Front made such sudden redeposits much more common, if still relatively unusual. An example of this was the excavation of the 'Heidenkopf' position in the German trenches at Serre. This loop of trenches bulging towards the British lines was considered by the Germans to be indefensible in the case of a large-scale attack. They therefore created a better defensive line some distance to the rear and planted four large mines below the 'Heidenkopf' itself. This was done by digging tunnels under the trench and placing charges at the ends. When the British attacked on the morning of 1 July 1916 these mines were blown. The result of this was that near the seats of the explosions large craters were created and the trench line was entirely destroyed. Slightly further away on either side of and between the craters the trench line was suddenly and almost completely backfilled within a few seconds with chalk rubble upcast by the explosions. Since it is known precisely when these explosions took place, the archaeologist has a snapshot below that chalk rubble of exactly what the condition of those trenches was when the mines went up. Fortunately for the German garrison, but unfortunately for the archaeologist, the occupiers of the trench knew the

Objects recovered from the battlefields on sale at a militaria fair in the UK. At least one rifle grenade is visible, as well as small arms rounds. Each object represents another small loss of unrecorded archaeological information. (*ASR*)

mines were about to be fired and evacuated not only themselves but any equipment they thought salvageable. (In fact they were not entirely successful. The defenders from 121 Reserve Infantry Regiment, along with some Pioneers, blew the mines, but were caught when they emerged from *Stollen II* ('Mine tunnel 2') to discover the British already in the German trenches behind them. German documentary evidence indicates that the commander of the party, Lieutenant Eitel, was killed, but no trace of the rest of the party was found when the Germans recaptured the area. It is quite possible that they remain entombed in *Stollen II*.) None the less, although the archaeologist's 'snapshot' was of an essentially empty, evacuated trench, the principle remains valid.

A similar situation prevailed at the site excavated at Loos. Here the whole area, another German salient known as the Hohenzollern Redoubt, had been subject to a sustained campaign of mining and counter-mining by both sides. Huge craters up to 30 feet (10 metres) deep had been blown repeatedly under the respective trench lines, and these craters in turn had been occupied and fortified as defensive positions in their own right. Unfortunately for the archaeologists, the repetition of this process over and over had created an area which was an enormous stirred-up mix of material that had been blown into the air any number of times. This presented an impossibly complex depositional sequence. No doubt careful excavation over a long period could unpick the stratigraphy of this site, but it was beyond the limited resources of the small-scale project team available at the time. Such explosively created archaeology is thus not always an advantage.

The force of an explosion also creates another difficulty not encountered in conventional archaeology. Normally each layer or context contains only the artefacts deposited at the same time – indeed, this is a key to understanding them archaeologically. Also the presence or absence of artefacts can be a useful guide to whether a deposit is anthropogenic (man-made) and thus an archaeological layer, or simply the pre-existing background soil (known as the 'natural' in archaeological parlance). Where the fill of a feature is made up of material very similar to the 'natural' the presence of objects can be the guide to which layer the excavator is in. Given that most Great War deposits contain metal debris, shell fragments, tins and the like to a varying degree, this was initially used as a guide.

Unfortunately this led to a problem. At Thiepval one of the trenches was backfilled with a highly compacted chalk layer. This was so similar to the natural chalk the trench was cut through originally that it was hard to distinguish between the two. A sweep with a metal-detector was used to determine whether further metal debris was present. Any response would mean there was still more backfill to remove, but otherwise the bottom had probably been reached. This was a technique that had been used successfully elsewhere. Unfortunately the responses on the detector continued to appear here, despite the fact that the diggers had reached what appeared to be solid chalk. How could metal debris get into the natural? The answer was uncovered fully 6 inches (15 centimetres) below the floor of the trench. A large (hand-sized) shell splinter had been driven into the floor of the trench with such force that it had buried itself that distance into the solid chalk. The conclusion was that bursting shells, and other explosions, were capable of distributing artefacts (shell splinters in this case) with such force that they would not only fall on to exposed layers but could also be driven through earlier deposits to come to rest in an entirely different deposit, or even the natural. Once again conventional archaeological wisdom had been overturned and the team was forced to think harder about the interpretation of the material.

A similar situation was encountered by a Belgian group (the Association for World War Archaeology) working on a medieval monastic site that had also been used as a dug-out by the British Expeditionary Force (BEF). On cleaning the section a clear disturbance could be seen passing through the clay and finishing below the foundations of the medieval building. Only when an unexploded German shell was found at the end of this trace could the disturbance be

The wall of a bunker excavated in Thiepval Wood. The track of an incoming shell is visible as a diagonal scar, along with a hollow, discoloured area where the shell burst. (*DRK*)

correctly interpreted: the Great War shell had inserted itself through the medieval layers and come to rest *below* them.

Such finds had an additional impact on the excavation team. To be confronted with the direct evidence of the enormous force created by such a shell burst, and the potential for destruction of metal fragments travelling at that speed, was sobering. The archaeology had once again offered a first-hand experience of a concept familiar to the excavators from books, but rarely as graphically expressed. This was not the only time the team members were thankful to be in the trench ninety years later, rather than at the time of its original occupation.

SAFETY

Discussion of explosions leads to a question commonly asked of the excavation team: 'Isn't your work terribly dangerous?' The answer to this is a qualified 'yes'. Over 1.6 million shells were fired on the 20 miles of the Somme front in preparation for 1 July 1916 alone. Over 4 million tons of munitions of all types were shipped to France from the UK during the war. Of the artillery shells used in the early part of the war in particular, perhaps as many as a third failed to explode when fired. This was either because they were fused incorrectly or they fell into soft ground, or they were 'duds' – poorly manufactured shells which simply didn't work properly. Thus many thousands of tons of unexploded ordnance remain in and under the green fields of France, waiting to be disturbed by the plough or by over-eager archaeologists.

Nor has the passage of time reduced the risk from these items, as the explosive mixtures they contain have not necessarily become less volatile with time. In fact the opposite is often the case, as explosives degrade into a *less* stable state as they decay. Casualties continue to occur every year as farmers and the unwary disturb sensitive items. As a number of recent press reports have shown, there are also people bold (or stupid) enough to collect and transport live munitions. There is a thriving (and entirely legitimate) collectors' market for safe munitions. Unfortunately this has led some unscrupulous people to deal in items which have either been 'made safe' informally in a Belgian garden shed, or worse, simply polished, painted and sold with their fuses or explosive content *in situ*. The risk to the buyer of these items, or indeed the other passengers on the ferry by which they return to the UK, requires little elaboration.

The best policy is thus to be very wary. Shells and grenades encountered in the field should *never* be touched unnecessarily. Indeed,

British gas cylinders removed from Thiepval Wood by the French Demineurs (Bomb Disposal Team), after discovery during the archaeological excavations. Two of them proved to be full of still-lethal gas. (*Ulster Tower*)

anything that is not immediately identifiable as safe should also be left alone. The heads of German stick grenades, once the stick has rotted, look just like food tins, and indeed some early grenades *were* made from food tins, packed with nails and explosives. Even material sold at fairs and markets should be treated with caution, and where possible disassembled and checked internally before any money changes hands. It must also be remembered that in the current security climate arriving at Dover with a Mills bomb on the parcel shelf will not make you popular with the authorities, and the argument that the Belgian farmer who sold it to you had already defused it may not carry much weight.

As archaeologists, however, the team members inevitably come into contact with large amounts of this material, and the risks for us remain as real as those to the general public (having an 'ology' is no protection against shell fragments). A balance therefore has to be struck between safety on site and managing the risks sufficiently to allow us to continue to work. All work is done with permanent on-site bomb disposal experts on hand, either from the armed forces or from civilian contractors, and their word is law. The moment any munition, or indeed any lump of rust

Stokes mortar rounds recovered during the Vimy excavations. The absence of paint means that explosive and chemical fillings cannot be easily distinguished. (*DRK*)

not immediately identifiable as safe, is found, the site is evacuated and the 'Explosive Ordnance Disposal' man is called in. Only after he has declared the item safe, or has carefully excavated and removed the object, does work resume. Sometimes this can be frustrating as the site is evacuated several times a day, but it is always better to be safe than sorry (and in any case archaeologists rarely refuse an opportunity for a quick tea-break so interruptions are not always unpopular!).

In addition to the explosive risk, there is also a significant danger from gas. All sides in the war used both lethal and non-lethal agents against their foes, either released along hoses from cylinders or packed into artillery shells. These agents remain just as dangerous today as they were when they were manufactured, and often their steel containers, be they shells or cylinders, have decayed significantly. All staff on site are briefed to be aware of any strange smells, and 'tell-tale' wind indicators made from fluorescent plastic tape hang from nearby trees. At the shout of 'Gas, Gas, Gas!', everyone moves rapidly upwind while the EOD people don full chemical protection suits to investigate.

Mostly our gas alerts have been precautionary or false alarms, such as when a Livens-projector tube (a type of gas-firing mortar) had been reused in a trench as a urinal. Precautionary alerts are common as Stokes mortar bombs, for example, come in both explosive and gas-filled types. Originally these were distinguished by painted markings, but once the markings have gone they are indistinguishable and all have to be treated as if gas-filled and removed accordingly. On one occasion the risk was very real, but the precautions worked well. In Thiepval Wood team members digging a newly opened excavation area uncovered the tops of some cylindrical objects. Examination of these by EOD revealed the daisy-wheel taps consistent with the tops of gas cylinders. They were far too dangerous to be lifted by the team, and there was no sensible choice but to shut down excavations entirely in that part of the wood, tape the area off and wait for the French bomb disposal teams to come in. In the event the French team arrived a week later armed with a mini-digger and full chemical protection gear. The area was cordoned off and the nearby road closed as they removed four cylinders of British 'White Star' gas (a lethal mixture of chlorine and phosgene). An alarming postscript to this story was the discovery that between us leaving the site and the French *Demineurs* arriving, an illegal metal-detectorist had visited one night and dug down to re-expose the cylinders, buried by the team for safety. The consequences of this not only for him but also for local residents (fortunately it's quite a remote area) could have been disastrous, and the incident illustrates the callous disregard for safety that some of these characters display.

THE CHALLENGE

The risks from gas and ordnance are only some of the challenges facing the Great War archaeologist. This chapter has shown that the archaeology itself is also highly complex. The depositional processes by which the archaeological remains were created were often significantly different from those of traditional archaeology, and the wide range of products and materials in use means that the taphonomic processes at work are highly variable. As a result the excavated evidence requires very careful examination and analysis to reveal all its secrets. Interpreting the excavated material is also made more complex by the wealth of documentary support available. The mass of photographs, maps and documents means that while some things are explained more easily, others produce curious problems and paradoxes which force us to reconsider both the excavated evidence and our interpretation of the documents.

In the following chapters it is hoped that the results of our excavations can be used to shed light on various aspects of the lives of the soldiers of the Great War, not only to illuminate or illustrate well-known features of the war, but also perhaps to challenge the received thinking about others, and maybe bring a new approach to some old preconceptions. It is also hoped that as the reader follows our trowels and tribulations across the Western Front, that journey is undertaken in the same spirit as the excavations themselves, as an act of remembrance and a (sometimes rather sweaty and physical) tribute to the lives of the men who fought the war. The final chapter remembers in particular four individuals whose lives were brought to the team's attention through the discovery of their remains. It is their stories, and more widely the stories of their millions of comrades in arms, which this book attempts to tell.

Chapter 2

Digging the Trenches

1914

It is one of the firmly held 'truths' of the Great War that in 1914 the belligerent forces were entirely unprepared for the character of the coming conflict. As with nearly all such ideas (as will become apparent in the course of this book), this is at best a half-truth and at worst a complete myth. Trench warfare had occurred before, notably in the American Civil War fifty years earlier, and more recently in Manchuria in the Russo-Japanese conflict of 1904–5. The fighting around Port Arthur in 1905 rapidly descended into an entrenched stalemate with much to teach an interested scholar preparing for modern warfare in 1914. At the time, however, prevailing doctrine saw these events as the exception rather than the rule. Almost all occasions of trench-based combat had taken place in the course of sieges of fixed strategic points, fortresses, harbours and the like. The use of sapping and mining in this context had been commonplace since medieval times, and was considered a separate art from the wider manoeuvre-based warfare, which it was assumed would characterise the greater part of any coming conflict.

The other major influence on the thinking of the BEF in particular was of course South Africa. The Boer War of 1899–1902 cast a shadow over all aspects of British military doctrine (insofar as the term was understood) in 1914 and indeed this is key to our understanding of how and why the British army of 1914 took the form it did. Many of the lessons of the South African conflict were well learned and contributed to the high level of expertise among British soldiers in 1914, and their realistic outlook. One of the most important lessons concerned the lethality of small-arms fire now that all infantry carried magazine rifles, and the killing power of the machine-gun (although these had not been deployed in large numbers in South Africa). The British soldier was thus accustomed to digging in in order to protect himself, and was equally experienced at assaulting entrenched positions. The latter lesson was learnt at high cost in 1899 when on several occasions the British launched traditional mass infantry assaults on entrenched Boers with the inevitable painful results. Incidentally, one of the great tragedies of 1914 in human terms is the fact that this lesson had not been learned by the French and German armies, and thus they had to learn it the hard way in 1914 at great cost in soldiers' lives.

In the BEF at least then, the soldier of 1914 was no stranger to the pick and shovel, and an entrenching tool formed part of his standard equipment. A pick-mattock had been available for issue in the late Victorian army, but this was not issued to all infantrymen. However, by 1908 the new Mills equipment provided all infantry with the means to carry the 'Implement, Intrenching, Pattern, 1908'. The French and Germans were equally equipped to dig, even if they had not had the same experience of its importance. The German tool was issued initially in 1874 and was general issue by the Great War. The French used the 'Pelle-pioche (Shovel/pickaxe/mattock) Seurre modele 1909' issued around that date.

The army had also issued the *Manual of Field Engineering, 1911*, published on 28 January 1911. This provided three pages on 'Improvement of the Field of Fire and Utilisation of Existing Cover', and a further eight pages on earthworks. The manual did not presuppose that trench warfare would develop on anything like the scale that it did, but the instructions for wiring, the layout of strongpoints (including redoubts) and of gun and machine-gun positions, all meant that the BEF had guidance on how to create virtually every individual component required for building extensive defensive positions. In the six-month

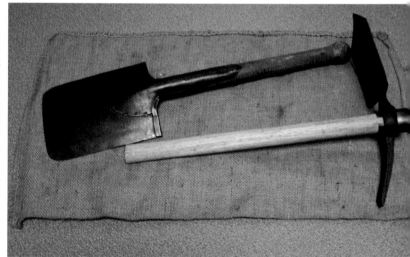

Examples of the standard British two-piece 'pick mattock' or entrenching tool. This was introduced in 1908 and used through both world wars. The German example was manufactured in one piece and was really a small spade. It had a reputation as a useful weapon in trench raids. (*ASR/RLC Museum*)

syllabus of training provided in *Infantry Training, 1914* (the standard manual for the training of troops prior to and during the war), no instruction in 'Entrenching' was provided for until the seventh fortnight, and then just for two hours out of the fifty-two available. A further three more hours followed in the eighth fortnight and a final three in the tenth fortnight, giving a total of eight hours in a six-month course. Thus, although it had formed only a limited part of his training, the BEF soldier had all the tools and instructions for trenching available to him in 1914, even if he had never before been asked to apply them on such a universal scale.

A summary of the basic information on field engineering, and entrenchment in particular, was also contained in one chapter of the 1914 edition of the *Field Service Pocket Book*. This book was intended as a handy guide for officers on all sorts of useful things from knots to camel convoys, and included information on trenches. As such it can be viewed as a summary of prevailing doctrine, and its first paragraph is instructive:

> 1. No natural or artificial strength of position will of itself compensate for loss of initiative when an army has time and liberty to manoeuvre. The choice of a position and its preparation must be made with a view to economising the power expended on defence in order that the power of offence may be increased.[6]

In short, the best form of defence is offence, and a trench is only an inferior and temporary expedient before the enemy is defeated by manoeuvre. In a sense this concept was to inform British trench construction right up to 1918 as it was always felt that trenches would only be required until the next 'big push', after which mobile warfare would return. To be fair to the often vilified generals, it must also be remembered that the Germans occupied a large portion of France and virtually all of Belgium for much of the war. Nor were they intending to give this territory back – Belgium was rapidly being incorporated into the 'Greater Germany'. Evidence of this policy was apparent to soldiers arriving at the front from Germany. By mid-October 1914 German reservists arriving at the Belgian border found themselves welcomed by signs to 'Neu Deutschland' (New Germany) that had been erected by the preceding German troops. One soldier described current thinking in a letter: 'The old people spoke Flemish which sounds like Low German. Flemish is simply another German dialect, all the more reason that this country must belong to Germany.'[7]

Thus, unlike the Germans, the allies could not win by staying put; the initiative to change the situation lay with them. A return to manoeuvre warfare was not so much an ambition as a necessity for winning the war. Trenches therefore were perceived as temporary constructions. The *Pocket Book* emphasises just how temporary with its advice that additional precautions should be taken if the position is to be held overnight. Interestingly the book disparages the notion of a continuous defence line, relying instead on defended localities with interlocking fields of fire, a doctrine that appears to have fallen out of favour for much of the war, only to be 'rediscovered' in 1917 and 1918.

What of the character of the trenches themselves and their archaeology? At their most basic the trench construction manuals of the period advocated a simple scrape in some cases as little as 6 inches (0.15 metres) deep, the size of a man, with the spoil (the dug-out soil) piled in front. This would offer rudimentary protection, and is about all a soldier might be expected to create using only the entrenching tool on his belt, especially if anyone was actively trying to kill him at the time. Photographs show all armies using this technique in 1914. Unfortunately these features are so slight that the chances of finding them archaeologically are virtually nil. A single season of ploughing, turning over the soils to a depth of over a foot (0.3 metres) would entirely obliterate them.

The 1914 manuals do also suggest more substantial constructions.

Belgian team members excavating 1914 period trenches at Bixschoote near Ypres. The extreme shallowness of these trenches is evident, as is the waterlogged nature of the surrounding land. *(DRK)*

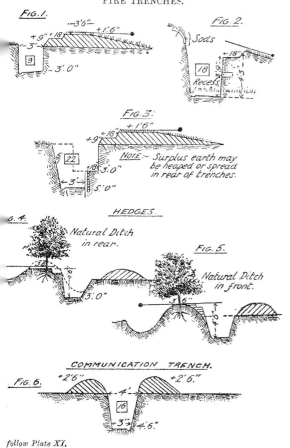

PLATE XII.
FIRE TRENCHES.

FIG.1.

FIG.2.

Sods

Recess

FIG.3.

NOTE:- Surplus earth may be heaped or spread in rear of trenches.

HEDGES.

Natural Ditch in rear.

FIG.5.

Natural Ditch in front.

COMMUNICATION TRENCH.

FIG.6.

follow Plate XI.

Illustration from the *Field Service Pocket Book 1914* showing suggested trench profiles, and the use of pre-existing ditches. The latter is not always a wise policy in low-lying areas like Flanders.

The simplest of these are shallow trenches up to 3 feet (0.9 metres) deep, while some are more complex and more closely resemble the familiar image of a trench, up to 6 feet (1.8 metres) deep and with a separate revetted fire-step. However, even the deeper trenches were not intended to form a connected system but were large enough to protect from as few as one or two men up to maybe a section of a dozen or so. Such trenches would be placed in an irregular pattern taking advantage of ground and natural cover. The use of hedge lines and existing ditches as cover is also recommended. The first winter of the war in Flanders and Artois was to demonstrate the folly of this latter policy – after all, those ditches had been dug there for a reason, and as winter came their natural function as drains became apparent.

Even these larger early trenches are difficult to identify archaeologically. In many cases the lines established in 1914 were to be held, lost and recaptured several times during the remainder of the war, leaving the original modest earthworks of 1914 subsumed into the much more substantial constructions of later fighting. Trench mapping and air photography in this early stage of the war were also in their infancy. Whereas in the case of, for example, the Somme battles of 1916 the archaeologist has a wealth of documentary data to guide him to the location of trenches, this is not so for 1914. The key therefore, if these early features are to be excavated, is to identify a section of line which is relatively well documented and rapidly fell out of use after 1914.

In this the *No-Man's-Land* team was lucky. As part of the work for *Finding the Fallen/Trench Detectives* in 2005 two sites were excavated in the corridor proposed for the construction of the A19 motorway around Ypres. In the event this new motorway was cancelled, but at the time it provided the spur for a substantial amount of archaeological work. Looking for a 1914 site, we approached our colleagues of the Belgian Association for World War Archaeology. This group, under the auspices of the West Flanders regional government, had conducted exhaustive research on the trench systems within the motorway corridor. Their work included the transposition of trench mapping and air photo data on to modern maps and so they were able to lead the NML team to a suitable section of line.

The trench selected lay just to the south-west of the village of Bixschoote, north of Ypres. Good air photographs existed of the site showing a German trench constructed in the autumn of 1914 but abandoned as they advanced in the spring of 1915. When it was subsequently excavated, several aspects of this trench were notable. The first was its shallowness. The high water table around Ypres is one of the reasons for the area's grim reputation, and many trenches in the area were built as 'command trenches' with soil heaped up in high parapets mostly above ground. Even by the standards of the salient these trenches were very shallow, the maximum depth below ground surface being only around 18 inches to 2 feet (0.5–0.65 metres). Modern ploughing had disturbed the ground to a depth of up to 18 inches (0.5 metres), so along most of the excavation area it was literally only the floor of the trench that survived. It was clear that even at this shallow depth the trench had been extremely muddy, with the underlying yellow clay rapidly turning to liquid. The floor of the trench was distinguishable by a band of trampled brushwood and building rubble, in particular roof-tiles that were probably scavenged from the farm complex immediately behind the trench. These had been placed along the floor in order to provide a drier footing. No evidence of trench-boarding ('duck-boards') was found, which suggests that the organised supply of trench stores had yet to develop.

Several large and broadly rectangular areas of deeper digging were revealed adjacent to the trench. These were perhaps 1 foot (0.3 metres) deeper than the floor of the trench and appeared to be the bases of dug-outs. 'Dug-out' is perhaps a bit of a misnomer in this case as the resulting structures would have been mostly above ground and would certainly not have been shell-proof, although they might have kept out air-burst shrapnel, which was the prevailing artillery ammunition of the time, 'Shelter' is probably a better description as they would have kept out the weather but little else. Interestingly, the shelters all appeared to have been cut on the rear of the trench, thus with their entrances facing towards the enemy. This practice soon fell out of favour as the war progressed, as such orientation left the dug-outs even more vulnerable to shelling, but in 1914 it may have seemed a sensible approach on the grounds that it did not interrupt the front – fighting – side of the trench.

Several rather mysterious deeper cuts were found during the excavation, one in particular apparently running through the floor of one of the dug-outs. On examination these cuts proved to be short lengths of trench that were deeper than the nearby German line, each measuring up to 3 foot 6 inches (1 metre) deep and up to 10 feet (3 metres) long; at the base they were little more than the length of a boot wide, with steep sides. A detailed examination of the history of the area showed that the first position occupied by the French in the area in 1914 was along the line of the excavation. This had been rapidly captured by the Germans and the line had stabilised with the French in a new position a few hundred yards to the south.

It is likely then that these deep cuts were the original French slit trenches, each capable of holding a few men, but unconnected with each other and of rudimentary construction. We had, rather by accident, stumbled upon some of the earliest trenches of the war. It was a fascinating and exciting discovery, given the elusiveness of such features. When the Germans had captured the line they had ignored these slit trenches and built a more substantial continuous line, filling in the earlier features with spoil from their own works. Happily for the excavation team, the Germans had not only filled in these trenches with spoil, but also dumped in them a range of battlefield debris, offering the archaeologists a fascinating collection of early German items.

One of the slit trenches produced a cache of six damaged but substantially complete leather *Pickelhaube* helmets, as well as a set of German belt order equipment with ammunition pouches, entrenching tool holder and water bottle. The high water table and local clay soil had left these items almost perfectly preserved. A rolled great coat was also found. As well as being fascinating artefacts in their own right, these objects have a poignancy in that they were probably discarded as their owners were either killed or wounded and no longer in need of them. Photographic evidence would also suggest that the *Pickelhaube* rapidly lost favour with German soldiers in favour of the soft *Mutze* cap, so it is

German *Pickelhaube* helmets found discarded in a disused early slit trench at Bixschoote, near Ypres. The waterlogged clay conditions left these objects in extremely good condition even after ninety years. (*DRK*)

possible that some soldiers took the opportunity of combat to 'lose' their spiked helmets.

The German material found in what were otherwise French-dug trenches also demonstrates one of the key principles in interpreting the archaeology of trenches. Very little of what survives within the trenches, unless it is on the floor or attached to the sides, can be reliably attributed to the occupants of the trench. All the time that trenches are in use they are kept essentially empty; only when they fall into disuse does material collect in them, and this can be misleading as to both the date and even the nationality of the trench. This is a trap for the unwary, and one of the many aspects of Great War excavations which serves as a lesson for traditionally trained archaeologists.

1915–1916

Despite the somewhat rudimentary nature of the first trenches of 1914, the trench system on both sides increased rapidly in sophistication from the first winter of the war through to the climactic battles of Verdun and the Somme in 1916. Developments on the Allied side were still tempered by the idea that a suitable offensive would push through the fixed defences, whereas the Germans knew they were there to stay and dug in with a vigour reflecting that determination.

The efforts of the archaeological team have focused largely on the Somme battlefields when examining trenches of this period. Several seasons of digging have been carried out on the German defensive lines at Serre, while a large-scale project continues on the British line at Thiepval Wood. Smaller-scale excavations were also carried out at Beaumont Hamel in 2005. These excavations have allowed us to develop an increasing understanding of the nature of the trenches in this area, their complexity and their dynamic character.

A fact often forgotten by English-speaking visitors to the Somme battlefields is that fighting did not suddenly start here in 1916. The German and French armies first clashed here in September 1914, and each developed an inter-dependent system of defences along what became a relatively quiet sector for the next year or so. The reorganisation and rationalisation of the distribution of British and French units along the Allied front in the autumn of 1915 placed the area in British hands at that time. Thus the trench systems on the Allied side of the wire were essentially French, subsequently modified to British specification. This 'layering' has to be borne in mind when the archaeology of these trenches is considered. In Thiepval Wood, for example, the trench system was sketched out in 1914 by the Germans, who then withdrew to a superior defensive position to the east of the wood. The French then took over the trenches, followed by the British (including the Ulster Division and some Indians). The area was abandoned in 1917–1918, then reoccupied by the Germans before they were finally driven out in the advance of August 1918.

The latest of these phases of occupation is potentially that likely to be best represented archaeologically, but features of all earlier 'periods' (to use archaeological terminology) are also to be found. A section of trench excavated at Beaumont Hamel, a battlefield famous for its part in the destruction of the Newfoundland Regiment on 1 July 1916, the 'First day of the Somme', produced a haul of over 800 British .303 rounds, fired and unfired. It also produced over 1,000 French *Lebel* rifle rounds dating from 1914–15, as well as dated rounds from 1918 and a button belonging to a New Zealand soldier who defended the area during the German offensive of March 1918. Thus the whole history of the site was represented artefactually. Visitors to the Somme area who assume everything they see is a product of the 1916 battles are making a significant mistake.

Even within each period of occupation the process of constructing new trenches and dug-outs was constant, as was the abandonment of redundant features. As part of the Thiepval Wood project an exercise known as 'map regression' was undertaken, whereby trench maps of as many dates as possible between 1915 and 1917 were compared, and the date of construction or abandonment of each section of trench was deduced from its appearance on or disappearance from the maps. The result was a complex web of different phases of activity as the system of trenches inherited from the French was adapted and remodelled. Interestingly, the names given to trenches can often be a clue to their date of construction, and who built them. While 'King Street' is fairly generic and tells us little of its builders, 'Govan', 'Clyde' and 'Sauchiehall' can fairly reliably be attributed to the 51st (Highland) Division (although in some cases they renamed existing French trenches), while 'Enniskillen Avenue' is likely to have been the work of their successors in the wood, the 36th (Ulster) Division. There is even a 'Meerut Street', named after the brigade of Indian cavalry that occupied the wood in late 1915.

Lancashire Fusiliers rehearsing an attack near Beaumont Hamel, 30 June 1916. The trench name-sign 'King Street' is visible, as well as a directional sign indicating the 'Firing Line'. A third sign board is also visible on the extreme right of the picture. (*Imperial War Museum: Q774*)

Trench maps only reveal this activity on the broad scale of whole trenches. The war diaries of the units concerned reveal a constant ant-like activity, as dug-outs were altered and rebuilt, new weapons including machine-guns and trench mortars were brought in and emplaced, and stores for the vast array of equipment and supplies were constructed. This is without allowing for the constant repairs needed after the ravages of enemy shelling and the weather. In short the greater part of a soldier's life in the trenches was spent digging, or carrying.

The trench systems of this period of the war were formed of a series of basic components, although each nation ordered these slightly differently and had varying ideas on the ideal spacing for the various lines and their detailed construction. Whatever nationality was involved, the basic function remained the same. The trenches had to be capable of both accommodating a garrison (which would live in them for days at a time) and providing firing positions. They had to be linked to the rear by communication trenches so that supplies and reinforcements could move up and the wounded be evacuated in daylight without attracting hostile fire.

The French experimented with a system of fighting trenches with a living trench close behind, in the hope that comfort could be combined with utility. This kind of system proved over-complex, difficult to maintain and a poor use of scarce labouring resources. The British army's approach was to have a front line supported by a shelter or supervision trench in which dug-outs were incorporated to improve the protection and comfort of the men not actually in the front line. The German solution was to stress the importance of the front line and reserve position, but with far great emphasis on the depth of dug-outs and the use of concrete throughout. By early 1916 German practice was to ensure that their dug-outs in the front line could survive direct hits from shells from all guns and howitzers up to 6 inch size (and up to 8 inch in reserve positions). German manuals took pains to discourage work that was too regular and neat and instead urged the construction of multiple new works rather than the over-elaborate and costly maintenance of old systems.

The use of material for trench revetment also demonstrated national characteristics. The French made extensive use of wicker hurdles, timber planks, branches, turf blocks and in some areas even stone or chalk. The German army used very little if any revetting in communication trenches, but emphasised the extensive use of timber and wicker construction in front-line trenches. Where they used sandbags, they aimed to avoid uniformity so domestic pillow-cases were mixed with manufactured 'earth bags', which were themselves of a variety of colours. As a result a German trench combined solidity with a jumbled external appearance which allowed sniper positions and other firing points to be more easily concealed. The British approach called for uniform sandbags and posts together with the extensive use of expanded metal and corrugated iron. As a result the British trenches were more uniform and regular than those of the French or Germans, and presented greater problems of concealment.

By early 1916 all the armies had adopted a generally similar system,

Team member Keith Maddison explores stone-built French trenches at Frise, on the high ground south of the River Somme. (*DRK*)

which featured a front, or firing, line supported by a reserve position linked by communication trenches and featuring dug-outs, weapons positions and latrines. Some 2,000–4,000 yards behind this front line was a second line with a similar layout. The distance between the lines provided a buffer to a successful breakthrough and meant that any attacker had to allow time to bring forward his field artillery (which had a range of about 7,000 yards) if he was going to assault the second line successfully. This took time and provided the defender with the opportunity to feed troops into the threatened sector sealing off the attack and preventing a breakthrough. At the time of the Somme offensive in the summer of 1916 the German troops were building a third line in case the Allied attack proved successful, as a means of localising any breakthrough. Although this line was not completed when the attack began, it provided a foundation for subsequent work and indicated the importance of defence in depth.

In the course of various projects the team has excavated a sample of each of these types of trench, from both sides of the wire, French, British and German. The following sections discuss what was found by digging each of these, and the functional and national differences which were encountered.

Front-line fighting trenches

The largest section of front-line trench excavated by the team to date is in Thiepval Wood. A section of trench about 15 metres long has now been cleared and restored to something like its original appearance. The area excavated represents one 'fire-bay' and one 'traverse'. Rather than being straight, those trenches intended for fighting or, as British trench maps describe it, 'apparently adapted for fire' were built with a series of kinks along their length. This was intended to minimise the effect of bursting shells within the trench, and to prevent enfilading fire along its length. Sections of 8–10 metres in length would typically form the forward fire-bays while the rearward traverses would be shorter, only 3–4 metres in length. Various designs were adopted, including square traverses forming a regular crenellated pattern, or V-shaped pointed ones. Naturally manuals show these features in an idealised fashion, evenly spaced along a straight trench. In reality fire trenches were much more irregular, although German systems when viewed on air photographs often appear more evenly spaced. This is not simply a measure of Teutonic efficiency, but a reflection that in many cases their defence lines were built on ground of their choosing, whereas the Allied lines tended to develop in whatever space faced the German position, avoiding local obstacles such as tree stumps and the like. After occupation for any length of time, damage from artillery and constant modifications for the installation of heavy weapons such as machine-

This section of the British front line in Thiepval Wood has been completely excavated and then restored with mesh revetting, a sandbagged parapet, and trench-boards. Here the setting is being explained to a school party by Teddy Colligan from the Ulster Tower. *(DRK)*

guns or mortars made these systems highly irregular and tortuous. A survey of the visible length of the front-line trench along the edge of Thiepval Wood proved this with angles and traverses appearing apparently randomly along the length of the trench.

Within each fire-bay the Thiepval front line is typically 5–6 feet (1.5–1.8 metres) below ground level. At the time of its construction this depth would have been enhanced by perhaps 2 feet (0.6 metres) of upcast spoil forming a parapet at the front and a parados to the rear. The deepest part of the trench was typically 2 feet (0.6 metres) wide, with a fire-step (a raised shelf along the front of the trench) of similar width. In Thiepval the natural chalk lies immediately below the topsoil so the trenches, while relatively hard work to construct, were fairly solid. In softer materials the sides would have to be revetted. This could be done using solid timber, although this was comparatively rare, or with expanded metal mesh or chicken-wire held in place with iron pickets. In French and German trenches woven wooden hurdles were frequently used. In German trenches this reflects the scarcity of metallic materials such as XPM (expanded metal mesh) and corrugated iron in comparison with the British. In Thiepval a mixture of XPM and chicken-wire was common, and seems to have been effective at retaining the coarse chalk rubble through which the trenches were cut. Fragments and some quite large sheets of both XPM and chicken-wire were encountered during the excavations. Sections of trench-board were also found, albeit in a very decayed state, but still recognisable at the base of the trench. These have been reproduced in the restoration of the trenches but were by no means ubiquitous as the solid chalk provided a firm, if somewhat slippery, footing.

Evidence of sandbagging was also uncovered. Occasionally in clayier materials the imprint of the weave of individual sandbags can be discerned. This was the case at Beaumont Hamel. At Thiepval, however, the chalk rubble was too coarse to retain these marks. None the less areas of sandbagging could still be recognised, as when the bags were filled each received a slightly different mix of fills and the resulting 'layer-cake' effect can be discerned in the excavated soils. Sandbags seem to have been used to reinforce areas where the trench walls were particularly weak (such as in areas of shell damage), rather than uniformly along the trench. The reason for this soon became apparent to the archaeologists restoring these areas, as building almost anything with sandbags is incredibly labour-intensive. Revetting with chicken-wire or XPM is much easier.

When viewed in isolation, the front line excavated at Thiepval seems like a substantial construction, but it was commonly accepted at the time and history generally suggests that German fire trenches were both larger and better-built than those of the Allies. In part this was due to the different strategic ambitions of the various powers, as discussed at the opening of this chapter. The view from the trenches that the 'grass was greener' on the other side of the wire may also reflect the fact that Allied troops were expecting to attack these defences. Rumours abounded of wallpapered dug-outs on the German side, with gramophones and even pianos. The truth was probably more prosaic, and generalisations are often unreliable, but the section of German line excavated at Serre supported this broad impression.

A portion of this line was examined in 2005. A section was cut across the German main line of defence south of the village. The trench in question, known as the *Bayern Graben*, in fact formed a second line behind a salient known as the 'Heidenkopf' (after its commander, Leutnant Heiden), but as the latter was only lightly defended the *Bayern Graben* was intended as the main line of defence in the area. Only a short length of the trench (about 12 feet, or 3.5 metres) was excavated

Excavation in progress on the German front-line trench at Serre. The large size of the feature is immediately apparent. The trench runs from bottom left to top right, and the chalky floor of the trench is visible. (*DRK*)

but this was sufficient to gain a cross-section of the feature. The trench itself was at least 10 feet (3 metres) deep and up to 13 feet (4 metres) wide at the top. No fire-step was uncovered but it is possible that the section excavated lay at the rear of a traverse, where no fire-step would have been constructed. This vast trench clearly demonstrated the impact of the bombardment during the Somme battle. The sides of the trench were poorly defined and sloped back at an angle, suggesting frequent collapse. None the less, even in its partially collapsed state the trench offered substantial cover and would have been a significant obstacle.

Communication trenches

While fire trenches tend to represent the typical trench in the public mind, it is arguable that they are the less common of the various forms. A glance at any trench map reveals that while a typical section of line might have two or three lines of fighting trenches, broadly parallel with the enemy's front, these would be linked by a vast network of communication trenches. As soon as a soldier entered an area under observation from the enemy lines he would be forced underground, and thus communication trenches normally started at a substantial distance from the actual front. On the Somme front the extent of German observation, in particular across the Ancre valley, forced communication trenches to be dug from up to a mile behind the line. The communication trench excavated by the team at Avril Williams' guest-house in Auchonvillers, a village nearly a mile from the front, connected into a trench known as 'First Avenue' and so on down to the front-line trenches opposite Beaumont Hamel.

Communication trenches were typically smaller than their fighting counterparts. Of those excavated none is more than 2–3 feet (0.5–0.75 metres) wide at its base, just enough for two men to squeeze past each other. If two large groups had tried to pass in opposite directions, such as during a relief, chaos would have ensued. This was avoided by using a one-way system with 'Up' and 'Down' trenches allocated prior to any large movement of troops. However, in the dark, or in the chaos of battle, wrong turns were common and it was not unusual for men to have to resort to the apparently dangerous practice of climbing out of the trench in order to get past each other. Communication trenches were also traversed on the same principle as fire trenches, but this tended to adopt more of a gentle zigzag pattern than the sharp crenellations of the front line.

The entrance to the cellar at Avril Williams' house in Auchonvillers. The brick flooring of the communication trench is visible on the left. (*DRK*)

Excavation has also uncovered evidence of revetting and trench-boarding in a similar fashion to that in the fire trenches. At Serre the team excavated a German-built communication trench running back from the *Bayern Graben*; it contained surviving *in situ* trench-boards at the bottom, and there were postholes cut into the chalk base, apparently to hold uprights for revetting materials for the sides. No surviving revetting was found, suggesting either that it took the form of woven hurdles which have not survived, or that any metallic materials used were subsequently salvaged. At Auchonvillers the communication trench excavated in the village was at least partly floored with quite carefully laid bricks salvaged from the nearby houses. This practice is also recorded in contemporary accounts, but it was not universally popular as the bricks could become extremely slippery in winter and unless very well laid were a constant trip hazard.

The other omnipresent feature of excavated communication trenches is telephone wire. Virtually all the trenches excavated have been strung with several strands, held against the side walls by metal staples driven into the earth. During the Great War the armies of all nations increasingly used radios or 'wireless', but their size and technical limitations meant that the majority of military messages were conveyed by telephone. The limitations of any system of communication which relies upon cables are obvious; it was necessary to lay and maintain the cables in an environment where shellfire or trench maintenance constantly severed links, while in an attack the troops rapidly moved beyond even the most advanced telephones in the network. These shortcomings explain why runners and carrier pigeons still had a vital role to play in the communication network.

At the beginning of the war telephones using Morse transmission rather than voice (which required more electrical energy) could send messages for up to forty miles, but it was usual practice to rely upon shorter links and have exchanges or relay stations to send messages over long distances. One technique for reducing the amount of cable required to establish telephone communication was the use of a single insulated cable to carry the outgoing signal. The telephones at both ends were then earthed into the ground by means of large copper spikes. The circuit was completed by the electrical impulses being carried through the wet ground. This 'earth return' system explains why single-strand cables can be found in some trenches, but these usually indicate early war telephone networks. By 1916, especially after the failure of British secrecy during the Somme battle, it was clear that 'earth return' systems offered the German army the opportunity to listen in to British military signal traffic simply by putting their own earthing rod into the ground. In favourable damp conditions, German intercept stations could pick up British telephone communication over 2 miles (3,000 metres) away.

As a result the British moved to a system utilising two insulated cables often bound together. At the same time efforts were made to improve the insulation of the wires, from a coat of enamel paint, which was easily scratched away, to types that included rubber coatings. This was combined with a change of wire away from the fragile early single-strand cable. Military cable began to use a strand of heavier gauge wire that was more resistant to snapping and being cut by shellfire. In some cases cables were 'looped and laddered' to provide multiple connections. The British even experimented with barbed wire and insulated rolls of chicken-wire as a means to provide a telephone link in no-man's-land. Although a single piece of shell fragment or stray boot could sever a cable, it was unlikely that every strand of wire in a width of chicken-wire sheet would be broken. The reactions of the signallers asked to unreel this into no-man's-land while under fire are unprintable.

Despite the improvements in field telephones, and the advent of more portable wireless sets (radios), semaphore, flags, signal lamps, pigeons and despatch-riders all played a role in Great War communication. Sadly for archaeology they do not leave behind the tell-tale cables, trenches and batteries of a telephone system, however simple. Although troops were meant to reel up old cable this was rarely done and became impossible as the war progressed and shelling became heavier, as by this time cables were frequently buried in purpose-dug cable trenches up to 6 feet (1.8 metres) deep. However, there was always a need for yet

A narrow communication trench at Beaumont Hamel, strung with multiple bunches of telephone wire, attached to the trench side with metal staples. Trench-boarding was present along the floor, but this was recorded and removed. (*DRK*)

another line and trenches remained strung with them, to the irritation of the soldiers who constantly snagged them and the signallers who had to repair them. At Beaumont Hamel trenches were found with several staples, each carrying multiple cables. It is likely that this was because the trenches excavated were adjacent to a brigade headquarters dug-out, and thus large numbers of lines would have converged at that point.

Support lines and specialist features

In addition to the trenches proper, a host of other underground features were constructed. These could accommodate virtually every military and domestic activity, from toilets to telephone exchanges, bomb stores to bath-houses. The universal space into which these facilities were squeezed was the 'dug-out'. This all-encompassing term is ascribed to features of all shapes and sizes, from a small room to a whole hospital, and of a varying degree of depth and safety.

The basic shelters of 1914 have already been discussed, but the lack of shell-proof protection these offered drove them rapidly out of fashion. Deeper structures were constructed. At least 10 feet (3 metres) of overhead cover was generally considered proof against all but the biggest shells. Two construction methods were available: 'cut and cover' or 'mined'. Cut and cover dug-outs were essentially a deep hole that was dug and then roofed over. These were acceptable when shallower spaces were required, and were often constructed with a complex layering of materials overhead: both soft layers of rubble or ballast to absorb shock, and hard layers to ensure the detonation of shells before they buried themselves too deep. Where the geology was suitable, however, as in the chalk at Thiepval Wood, it was found to be easier to 'mine' dug-outs, that is to cut the space directly out of the solid rock, leaving the material overhead *in situ*. Only the spoil from the interior space of the dug-out itself needed to be removed and this approach was found to be less labour-intensive.

The danger inherent in men trusting to the protection of old shallow dug-outs was recognised, and orders forbidding their use were issued. In Thiepval Wood a feature has been excavated which was likely to have been one of these shallow dug-outs. It took the form of a rectangular pit cut into the chalk to a depth of about 8 feet (2.5 metres). Planking was found in the base suggesting it had once been roofed, but at some point after 1916 (a British shrapnel helmet having been found in the fill) it was deliberately filled in and a subsequent trench line cut through the backfill. It is possible that the backfilling was intended to place the dug-out beyond use, but it is equally likely that a disused dug-out was a useful place to dispose of spoil from more recent excavations.

Indeed, the disposal of spoil from any new trench workings was a constant problem, especially in chalk areas. New spoil would show up clearly to the enemy and attract fire, and so dumping in an old dug-out was ideal. At Serre the team found a shell hole filled with large clean chalk blocks, sandwiched with a series of layers of topsoil. A range of German dug-outs and mine tunnels were built in the area, and it is likely that this chalk was the spoil from deep mining. Each night chalk would be dumped in the hole and covered with dark soil to camouflage it before morning. Next night there was another dump and more soil, producing the layered effect found archaeologically. Even these techniques, however, could not keep up with the mass of material produced, and at Thiepval Wood documentary sources record spoil being carried out to the rear in sandbags by working parties, in the process providing a ready source of filled bags for another field engineering task.

In villages and other built-up areas pre-existing underground spaces were also utilised. A nice dry cellar was the abode of choice of many a soldier, although often these were not as deep as a purpose-built dug-out. One way to increase the overhead protection was to deliberately demolish the building overhead, as rubble afforded far better shell-proofing than a standing building, but this was unlikely to have been popular with any remaining local inhabitants. A further alteration made to cellars adapted for use as dug-outs was the addition of a second entrance. In shelled areas the risk of the way out being blocked by a shell was very high, so a second exit, no matter how rudimentary, was always constructed. The cellar of Avril Williams' guest-house, which was utilised in this way during the war, shows evidence of a second door, the tunnel to it blocked in by a post-war repair. When such places were full of men, the second exit also assisted with the flow of air, although not to any great extent, as both structural cellars and purpose-built dug-outs were notorious for their airlessness, their extremes of either heat or cold, and their dampness. The evocative but somewhat loosely defined adjective 'frowsty' was coined to describe this atmospheric phenomenon and occurs frequently in the literature.

Before moving on from the cellar in Auchonvillers, we should consider its function. Visitors invariably ask 'what was it used for in the war?' as

Avril Williams' cellar at Auchonvillers. The chalk blocks of the walls are carved with the graffiti of successive soldier-occupants, including several stretcher-bearers, as well as members of the 36th (Ulster) Division. (DRK)

if there were a simple answer to this question. Perhaps they imagine that
the place was taken over, assigned a specific role and carried on in that
way for four-and-a-half years! This accords with the highly static
concept of the fighting which characterises the popular perception of the
conflict. It is far more likely, and would have been equally the case with
dug-outs built closer to the front line, that the function of the cellar
changed as different armies, and different units within those armies,
moved through the area. What suited one unit as a headquarters might
have served another simply as a store; evolution was constant, change
rather than stability being the keynote.

An excellent example of this phenomenon was excavated at Beaumont
Hamel. A rectangular feature was uncovered, approximately 6 feet (2
metres) square and 5 feet (1.6 metres) deep. The sides were supported by
corrugated iron sheeting, held in place by angle-iron posts. Although the
feature was completely backfilled, no evidence was uncovered of a roof
or any form of overhead cover. As the team dug down further a length
of iron tube was uncovered; this caused a certain amount of concern as
a battery of 'Livens projectors' (primitive mortars used for firing gas
canisters) was known to have been based in the area. In the event the
tube turned out to be innocent, simply a length of pipe pushed into the
floor of the pit in order to serve as a urinal. Next to it, set on a neatly
tar-papered floor, was a standard British Army latrine bucket. We had
uncovered a trench toilet. Continued excavation below the tar paper,
however, revealed a square recess in the centre of the floor,
approximately 3 feet (0.9 metres) square, and filled with clay bearing the
clear imprints of sandbags. Such a recess was an absolutely standard
feature of a trench-mortar pit, the sandbags providing a stable support
for the mortar base-plate. Thus we also had a mortar pit. The obvious
conclusion was drawn that the feature had started life as a mortar pit,
although these were by their nature only occupied for short periods as
they drew retaliatory fire from the Germans, hence mortar crews moved
position frequently. After the departure of the mortar it was obviously
decided that this unoccupied space, which was well ventilated and open
to the air, unlike a dug-out, would make an ideal latrine. A further
element was added to this puzzle by the discovery within the clay used
to fill the sandbags in the recess of several medical items, including a tin
of iodine ampoules and part of a thermometer. Whoever had filled the
sandbags had done so with material previously occupied by a medical
post of some sort, thus recycling and relocating the objects. It would be
an easy conclusion to suggest that the mortar pit position was also used

A mortar pit at Beaumont Hamel that was subsequently re-used as a trench latrine, with the latrine bucket and tar-paper floor still *in situ*. Corrugated iron revetting is also clearly visible. (*DRK*)

as the medical post, but the fact that the items were found within the fill of a sandbag suggests that they were imported to that particular spot *in* the sandbag, although it is unlikely that they came from far away. Such is the complexity of deposition and redeposition encountered in Great War archaeology.

1917–1918

As the war progressed trench design continued to evolve, and became ever more sophisticated. A section of the British line to the north of Ypres was excavated by the team in 2005. This trench formed part of the front line of July 1917, the jumping-off point for the Third Battle of Ypres, engraved on the popular memory as 'Passchendaele'. The difficulties with drainage and the nature of the ground around Ypres have already been alluded to earlier in the chapter. The trenches excavated at Forward Cottage provided evidence of how these problems were tackled but not necessarily overcome. Due to the soft ground, the trenches were lined throughout with corrugated iron. This made the line of the trenches relatively easy to see during excavation. Once the topsoil had been removed, the trench was visible as a darker line in the underlying clay and the rusted corrugated iron showed as a thin orange line in the soil on either side of the fill of the trench. Once excavated, the iron was clear to see, although it was highly corroded. The amount of iron sheeting needed for even a short length of trench was stark proof of the logistical effort required to sustain the fighting at this stage of the war, and it is unsurprising that the Germans by this stage were making wide use of more easily obtainable wooden hurdles as iron became increasingly scarce.

Holding the corrugated iron in place was a perennial problem. On the Somme, and in other areas where the ground was relatively firm, a picket could simply be driven into the floor of the trench and anchored with a wire attached to a peg buried under the parapet. At Ypres, however, the soft ground rendered this impossible. The solution was another classic design feature of trench architecture, the A-frame. This consisted of four pieces of timber baulk, typically 2–3 inches (5–8-centimetres) in cross-section. These were attached together to form a flat-topped 'A' shape, which was then inverted into the trench. The long arms held back the

Trench-boards excavated at Forward Cottage near Ypres. In addition to the lower board in the foreground, at least four subsequent layers of boards are visible in section, encased in mud. (*DRK*)

sheeting on the sides of the trench at a slight outward angle, while the central cross-piece braced the two sides apart. A trench-board could then be laid across the central brace from one A-frame to the next. This had the effect of raising the boards some way off the floor of the trench and providing a drain beneath. This no doubt seems excellent in principle and no doubt worked well, but one can also imagine the reaction to a boot breaking through a rotten trench-board to disappear into the void beneath, or small objects dropped between the slats of the trench-boards to be lost for ever in the mire below.

Such are the preservative conditions of the waterlogged clay of the salient that in many cases the timber of these A-frames was well preserved and readily revealed by excavation. As is always the case, however, the practice was always more difficult than the theory, and in many areas we found frames that had been repaired with additional cross-braces, or with further layers of trench-boards added as the level of the mud rose. In one area as many as five separate layers of trench-boards were uncovered, each simply laid on top of those below, as digging the earlier ones out of the mud was considered too difficult.

In addition to the developments in the detailed techniques of trench construction, the later years of the war also saw an evolution in the overall design of defensive systems. The German army studied hard the fighting on the Somme in 1916 and by November, influenced by the experiences of their attack at Verdun and their tenacious defence on the Somme, German policy called for the second line, and successive positions, to be up to 6¼ miles (10 kilometres) behind the front, providing a deep buffer zone in which any attack could be dealt with. This would be the work of both the reserve forces sent to the area from behind German positions and also the garrison of the zone between the two positions, who were provided with fortified villages, redoubts and centres of resistance to slow and funnel the enemy attack. By the end of the war the orthodoxy of front-line, support and reserve trench systems linked by communication trenches had been replaced by a more dispersed system of redoubts and defensive positions, the use of individual shell holes and great emphasis on concealment and flexibility. Emphasis was now placed on redoubts using natural features such as hills or quarries as the basis for their defence. This gradual move to defence in depth and dispersal of fortifications is an indication of the way in which weapons and tactics of all armies had adapted to the nature of warfare and help to demonstrate that the accepted view of the Great War as one that was fought entirely in trenches is inaccurate.

When the new defences of the *Siegfried Stellung* (known to the British as the 'Hindenburg Line') were constructed in the winter of 1916/17, these lessons were incorporated. It had been realised that no matter how strongly it was constructed, a well-supported infantry attack would almost always penetrate the front line of a defensive system. Thus, rather than hoping to halt the opponent in no-man's-land, a new policy was developed of layered defence, which assumed from the outset a degree of penetration by the enemy. The analogy may be drawn between an egg, which relies on its impenetrable hard shell, and a sponge, with its ability to absorb pressure. The new German defences had a relatively thinly held front line, behind which attackers would be drawn into a ground selected by the Germans, covered by interlocking machine-gun strong-points and pre-registered artillery. This had the additional advantage that their own artillery need only to range on to ground within their own positions and could thus be placed further back out of reach of the Allied guns.

This deeper system did not, however, mean that the defences themselves were any less substantial. The Hindenburg system (to call it a 'line' is somewhat misleading) included trenches quite as large as any seen on the Somme the previous year, and concrete was used very extensively to create strong-points and reinforce dug-outs. A similar system was also developed in the north at Ypres. Here concrete was particularly useful as it allowed pillboxes and other emplacements to be constructed at ground level yet still be shell-proof, as deep digging for shelter from artillery was difficult because of the ground conditions.

The later fighting of the Passchendaele campaign was characterised by the struggle for these concrete positions, each remaining intact in an otherwise utterly destroyed landscape, and having to be individually captured in bitter platoon and company level fighting. The excavations at Forward Cottage proved that even in this apparent wilderness of destruction coherent trench systems survived to be identified archaeologically. But for the casual visitor the concrete emplacements dotting the landscape are the most visible relic of the Flanders battlefields, some standing incongruously in the middle of fields grazed by cattle, others subsumed into post-war houses or converted to more peaceful uses.

This defensive development is often regarded as an exclusively German phenomenon. However, as with the evolution of methods of attack, in fact these new techniques were quickly adopted by both sides. After the collapse of Russia in 1917, freeing large numbers of German troops for the Western Front, it was clear to the Allied commanders that they would have to withstand a substantial attack before they could return to the strategic offensive. A programme of defensive works was therefore put in train along very similar 'deep defence' lines to those built earlier by the Germans. In the event this system was neither fully constructed nor sufficiently strongly manned when the main German blow fell in Operation *Michael* in March 1918, and as a result large sections of the defences on the British Fifth Army front were rapidly overrun. However, the scheme was correct in its conception, if not in its application.

The fighting following the March offensive of 1918, the so-called *Kaiserschlacht*, took the opposing forces back across the Somme battlefields of 1916, and this has added yet another archaeological layer to what is already a complicated picture. As in Flanders, the most obvious legacy of this campaign is in concrete. A number of concrete posts can be seen across the Somme area, and while some of these are part of the 1916 systems others were built in 1918. One such post, at La Signy Farm to the west of Serre, was excavated in 2004.

A concrete 'flash-spotting' post excavated at La Signy Farm near Serre. Probably dating from 1918, this post may have replaced an earlier less permanently constructed position. (*DRK*)

It proved to be a keyhole-shaped structure with a semi-circular, domed front portion with a vision slit, connected to a tunnel leading back to an entrance off a trench to the rear. The post had a distinctive, wide vision slit in its front face, leading to speculation that it was a 'flash-spotting' post. Flash-spotting was a technique whereby Allied observers would note the bearing and time of flashes of German guns firing behind their lines. Bearings from several posts could then be compared and the position of the German gun triangulated, allowing for retaliatory bombardment. A similar process using microphones to triangulate the sound of guns firing, known as sound-ranging, was also used.

A memoir by one such flash-spotter describes a sound-ranging post he occupied in 1916: it 'lay under a hedge corner just south of Ligny (*sic*) Farm, facing Serre'.[8] This location corresponds well with our excavated post, so the two may well be one and the same. However, in 1916 this position was simply splinter-proof with some cover, but the location was ideal for establishing the position of enemy guns as it was close to the front line and had an extensive field of view towards enemy territory.

Construction of the later concrete emplacement had clearly been quite hasty as much of the exterior of the structure bore the negative imprints of sandbags, where these had been piled against still-wet concrete. This effect can be seen even more strikingly on two posts on the road between Auchonvillers and Mesnil, where the structures were clearly made using internal wooden shuttering but with the wet concrete retained on the

This concrete post near Auchonvillers was one of several facing towards Beaumont Hamel on the Mesnil road. The impressions of the sandbags used to retain the wet concrete are clearly visible. (*DRK*)

Andy Robertshaw explores a German bunker forming part of the *Siegfried Stellung* defensive system near Cambrai. (*DRK*)

outside by a sandbag wall. The surface created once the sandbags have eroded away is particularly distinctive.

The other noticeable feature of the La Signy post is its location, as it was built into an existing field boundary lynchet, with observation down a shallow valley running away to the north-east. The deep defence system of which this formed a part relied on terrain to create fields of fire and to deny the enemy easy observation of defended areas. As with all forms of archaeology, the landscape context of these structures is as important to their understanding as their structural detail. A surviving trench map from early 1918 shows an observation post in a location corresponding with the excavated post, and indicates it is part of an elaborate system of interconnected defences stretching across the landscape. As an aside, an interesting feature of this defence is the inclusion of anti-tank guns, positioned close to the front for direct fire. We now know with hindsight that the Germans never developed an effective tank arm, but in 1918 that fact was by no means obvious. As we copied their systems of defence, there was no reason to think they would not copy our key weapons of offence.

This chapter has shown that not only were there a huge variety of trenches and other excavated features on the Western Front at any one time, but that these were constantly being improved, altered and redesigned as technology and tactics changed through the war. The idea that the front was static and unchanging is clearly erroneous. A reading of any of the many published soldiers' memoirs shows that they remembered each year from 1914 to 1918 as having its own distinctive character. This is also the case archaeologically, and provides not only the complexity but also the historical richness of excavation of the Western Front.

Chapter 3

Living in the Trenches

TRENCH ROUTINE

Once the trench lines had been established, as described in the previous chapter, it fell to the soldiers of the infantry to garrison them. It is a common misconception that once soldiers entered the line they stayed there for long periods. In fact this was not the case. In each sector of the line allocated to a British infantry division (which can be calculated as being between 5,000 and 7,000 yards depending upon the nature of the ground to be held) the divisional commander would put two brigades in the line at any one time, with the other brigade 'resting' in reserve. This euphemism meant that they were available to supply the units in the front line by carrying endless stores up the communication trenches, repairing roads and digging cable trenches, while fitting in training and other tasks until their turn for front-line duty came round. In a quiet sector front-line duty could be preferable to the drudgery of being in reserve. In the same way that the brigades were rotated, so were the battalions in the brigade, so that usually two infantry battalions (there were four of these per brigade initially, later reduced to three) would take turns holding the front and reserve trenches. At battalion level the organisation into four companies usually meant that two were in the front line facing the enemy at any one time. During the day one man in ten was on guard duty and at night this was increased to one in three. During the day men could clean themselves and their kit and weapons, eat and sleep, as it was warmest in the afternoon. Night-time activities included trench and barbed wire repairs, carrying out patrols and relieving men who had been left in the dangerously isolated listening posts out in no-man's-land.

As a result only a fraction of the strength of an infantry division was actually in the front line. During the day an observer watching from an aircraft would have been hard put to see any sign of the trench garrison other than drifting smoke from a carelessly attended cooking fire, the glint of a sentry's trench periscope mirror and a few bits of rubbish thrown over a parapet. This did not mean that even this activity went unnoticed and sentries and snipers were constantly vigilant for the mistakes of the opponents. All too often this lack of attention had fatal results. The last words of the writer H.H. Munro ('Saki') were 'Put that bloody cigarette out' before he was felled by a German sniper near Beaumont Hamel.

Due to these arrangements the time most soldiers spent a few hundred yards from the enemy would be brief as relief would be due every few days. By 1916 a spell in the trenches of more than a few days without going to the rear to recover and rest was to be commented upon. In the same way that divisions relieved and replaced their elements, be they brigades, battalions or companies, a general relief, which saw the division or corps being replaced in its entirety, was not infrequent. In consequence replacement units would arrive either from reserve or from another sector and the formation they replaced would march or be transported elsewhere on the front, taking their turn with more resting, training, processing the constantly arriving reinforcements, or even being sent by train or ship to another theatre of war.

Men of the Army Service Corps celebrate Christmas behind the lines in Salonika. Similar scenes of merry-making were not infrequent among men who were given the opportunity to enjoy themselves away from the trenches. (*RLC Museum*)

In addition it must be remembered that these infantrymen represented only the 'sharp end' – the tip of a very large iceberg. Large numbers of men in khaki or field grey never went near a front-line trench, although this is not to suggest that these men had an any less important role, or indeed that they were out of danger as many worked within reach of artillery fire behind the lines. However, they were not in the trenches *per se*. Of the 2,047,000 men and women in the British army during November 1918 roughly 42 per cent were in the 'teeth' arms of infantry, cavalry, tanks and machine-gunners. Of the remainder slightly less than half were in 'support' arms, such as artillery and engineers, and rather more than half were 'service' or logistics troops, including drivers, cooks, labour corps, and the like. This means that the ratio of combatants to non-combatants was 1 to 2.5. The majority of these service troops never saw a front-line trench and few ever had to venture into them.

Support troops had detachments in the trenches as forward observers or in the case of engineers supervising field works or doing specialist tasks. For this group the experience of the trenches was likely to be brief and occasional, as they did not form part of the permanent garrison supplied by the infantry and supplemented by cavalry serving on foot. This meant that many engineers were engaged in tasks such as running railways that meant that they too would never venture into the front line. This should not be taken as meaning that over half the army was safe; they may not have been in the front line but they still risked death from shelling, bombing, gas and accidents. It is also worth saying that many ex-infantrymen were transferred to labour battalions if they were medically downgraded as a result of wounds. At the same time many Army Service Corps officers, for example, transferred into 'teeth' arms, including the Royal Flying Corps, as the need for experienced and trained officers grew. At the same time the Army Service Corps provided drivers for the first tanks. None the less, the point is that the majority of soldiers who served in the Great War did not share the worst experiences of trench warfare, and even those in combat units were not expected to man the front lines for extended periods.

Large-scale combat, the 'big push', was also the exception rather than the rule. Set-piece battles for much of the war were relatively unusual events requiring an enormous degree of planning. They occurred infrequently along the front as a whole, and in a particular sector only a few times in the whole war. Some particularly quiet areas saw no large-scale combat at all. Thus an infantry soldier might find himself involved in several months of frequent combat, during a large battle such as the

Somme or Ypres, and then his division might move out of the offensive zone into an area where for as many months very little fighting happened.

One of the author's grandfathers might be taken as an example. Private 41957 John Andrew Robertshaw served in the British army from April 1916 until he was demobilised in March 1919. During this time he participated in the closing stages of the battle of the Somme, but did not attack. He was in reserve during the opening days of the battle of Arras in April 1917 and went into action for the first time in May of the same year on Greenland Hill near Arras thirteen months after he was conscripted. Wounded in this attack, he was hospitalised but later returned to his unit, the 12th Manchesters, in time to go into attack on Greenland Hill again in September 1917. Wounded again, he was evacuated to the United Kingdom and returned to France this time in the ranks of the 10th East Yorkshire Regiment. Following an extensive Lewis-gun course he arrived with his unit in the line just before the German spring offensive of April 1918. This was the longest period of combat in which he was engaged, largely because he avoided injury until being wounded again in August of that year during the battle of Amiens and the advance that followed.

Private John Andrew Robertshaw (grandfather of the author), photographed with his parents, brother and sister. A volunteer of April 1916, he was wounded three times, once severely, and served in three regiments. He fought in the later stages of the battle of the Somme, at Arras in 1917, and then against the German spring offensive before being wounded for the last time during the '100 Days' of 1918. (*ASR*)

With time out of the line, resting, additional training and time in hospital, Private Robertshaw was 'in action' for a fraction of his time in service. His total time with the British army was thirty-six months, of which just over five months was after the Armistice in November 1918. A further five months was spent in training in the United Kingdom and France. This leaves just over two years of potential active service. During this time he was in hospital for about a month between mid-May and late June 1917. Then he was wounded so severely that he was evacuated to England from late September until about Christmas of the same year, roughly three-and-a-half months. His final wound meant that he missed the closing months of the war and he was still recovering from a wound received in August 1918 when the war ended. These seven months of hospitalisation reduced his opportunity for service with the two infantry units to which he belonged to rather less than nineteen months. If we deduct time spent doing additional training (he became a Lewis-gunner in early 1918), the available time is a little more than a year and a half, during which time, despite never being eligible for leave, he missed the battle of the Somme, was in reserve at Arras in April 1917 and was wounded and in hospital at the time of Passchendaele. However, he was in the thick of the German offensive of March 1918 and the early stages of the final Allied offensive. He can be counted to have gone 'over the top' twice in minor attacks or raids in 1917 and then not again until August 1918. His career cannot be remarked upon as being 'easy' but it certainly indicates the relative infrequency of the classic battle in a typical infantry soldier's career.

It was recognised that in long periods of action the performance of units deteriorated, not only through casualties but also through widespread strain and fatigue, and thus some effort was made to rotate units in and out of combat areas. Unfortunately this process was hindered by the fact that some divisions developed a particular reputation as good troops and would therefore be called upon to fight far more often than their less renowned colleagues. Having a good fighting reputation as a brigade or division was thus definitely a two-edged sword. One of the reasons for the overall success in the war of the British army was its increasing ability to mount offensives rapidly one after another. This developing ability (known among military historians as 'tempo') allowed the BEF in 1918 to deliver blows against the Germans in rapid succession on different parts of the front, not allowing the enemy time to recover or bring up reserves. One unfortunate side-effect of this was that while each offensive was individually less costly than those of 1916 or 1917, owing to improved fighting techniques, their frequency made the overall casualty rate month by month the highest of the war.

Combat itself, however, is a subject for a later chapter. The purpose of this section is to consider how life was lived by a soldier in the trenches when he was not fighting, and what additional light can be shed on that life by archaeological excavation. How did he take care of all the domestic chores which in peacetime are taken for granted as part of normal life? How would a man eat, sleep, keep clean and look after all the rest of what the modern army calls 'personal administration' during his tour in the front line? Among all this domestic detail it must be remembered, however, that the business of killing continued at a low level as a constant backdrop; men were killed and wounded every day in a typical tour from shelling, sniper fire and other perils. Thus all of the activities described in the following sections were defined and constrained by the necessity of staying hidden, and avoiding the attentions of the enemy.

THE DAILY ROUND

The chief functions of troops in the front-line systems on both sides of the wire in a quiet sector were pretty similar. First, they were to guard the position against enemy attack; secondly, to improve where possible their own defensive position; and thirdly, to interrupt the enemy as far as possible in his efforts at both of the former. The extent to which efforts were made to disrupt the enemy again depended on the aggressiveness of the formation, be it battalion or division. Some units took it as a matter of pride to dish out as much suffering to those opposite as possible, while others were more tranquil. Much is made by some historians of the 'live and let live' attitude and Christmas truces and such, whereas in fact things were much more informal and less altruistic. Troops rapidly learnt that stirring up the enemy simply resulted in 'tit-for-tat' trouble for one's own side and so they left well alone. Unfortunately this went against the declared policy of the higher commanders, although phrases such as 'dominating no-man's-land' are much easier to express at headquarters than to carry out in a trench, and a good deal of friction resulted as the urgings of the commanders were widely ignored in the line. It wasn't unusual for troops about to be relieved from front-line duties to carry out a vindictive trench raid or mortar bombardment on the enemy in the hope that any retribution would fall on the men taking over the line rather than on the perpetrators. When the 51st Division was withdrawn from the trenches around Thiepval in January 1916 the quietness of the preceding period was remarked upon. The divisional history recorded 'There had been no infantry action beyond a few encounters between patrols', but as the Highlanders were leaving 'a small bombing raid [was] carried out by 154 Brigade on 2nd January 1916'. The raid took place the day before the Highlanders were to be relieved, so no doubt they knew that any retaliation would be visited on their successors.

Moments of violence apart, the daily routine was relatively consistent, and may be said to have begun at dawn with 'Stand-To'. It has been a tradition for some time that a likely time for attack is first thing in the morning. Thus as dawn broke each day all the men in the front line would take post along the parapet in case of such an attack. This might be accompanied by a few pot-shots at the enemy, who was likely to be doing the same thing, but generally finished after a short period. While no attack was necessarily expected, this practice also served as a general daily test of readiness and as an equipment check.

After stand-to most men would fall out but a few sentries would be left to keep an eye on the enemy. For the remainder the day was spent in a variety of chores, both personal and collective, such as repairing the trench, cleaning kit, washing, and preparing and eating food. However, as was alluded to above, stand-to can only be considered the start of the day in the loosest sense. In fact the hours of daylight tended to be the quieter part of any 24 hours. Most large-scale activity such as trench repair, wiring, carrying parties, or indeed raiding the enemy was carried out at night under the cover of darkness. Quite often the day was the

Cooking in a reserve trench, Ypres, March 1917. The men to the rear are probably members of a working party, hence the baulk of timber carried by one man. Note the old hedge and ditch on the left and the above-ground 'Command' parapet on the right. (*Imperial War Museum: Q4840*)

only time when a soldier might catch a little sleep or sort out his own affairs, do his own washing, cooking, etc. Inevitably this would be interrupted by duties of all kinds so a tour in the front line, be it for 48 hours or a week, was usually notable for the lack of opportunity to gain more than an hour or two of sleep each day.

As night fell, the trench system would come alive like a giant ant-hill as all sides set about their various tasks. Principally for the ordinary soldier this meant digging or carrying, or digging and carrying away the spoil! It must be remembered that the men in the front line had to be supplied every day with a vast array of supplies, not only ammunition and food but also timber and trench building materials, tools and, heaviest and most vital of all, water. It is often forgotten in the rather muddy popular image of the war that the lack of clean water to drink or wash with was a perennial problem; what little was available was carefully husbanded and used as sparingly as possible. Thus each night those men rotated out of the line in reserve or support, or what was ironically known as 'rest', would be called upon to fall-in as beasts of burden to carry the vast assortment of typically heavy or bulky stores forward through the trenches to forward dumps and front-line positions. In bad weather or under enemy shellfire even short distances became hugely difficult and men could easily spend all night on a single journey.

FOOD

The result of all this effort by the carrying parties was that contrary to popular myth the men in the front line were generally fairly well provided with the necessaries of life. Food in particular, although dull was seldom scarce. British rations had a heavy emphasis on meat

A typical British petrol or water tin found in Thiepval Wood. The fact that such tins could be used for both water and fuel led to the often petrol-tainted tea recalled in many memoirs. (*DRK*)

(fresh or preserved), bread or biscuit, plentiful if ill-tasting sweet white tea, cheese and jam. With a diet providing over 4,000 calories per day, the British soldier serving on the Western Front certainly did not starve. It was found very early in the war that young soldiers in particular rapidly put on weight when undergoing basic training, not only in response to the amount of food provided, but also in contrast to the food shortages many had suffered as civilians.

Although the type and quantity of rations did vary over the course of the war, and in some cases rations were not issued in sufficient quality or quantity during periods of intense fighting, the British soldier faced a significant problem with what he was issued. This was an excess of the most basic ration, tinned meat, in the form of 'bully beef' (tinned corned-beef) and tinned rations of meat and beans ('Maconochies'). These were frequently discarded, surviving in their tins to be found by unwary archaeologists to this day, or were given away to civilian children by soldiers on the march. The call for 'Bully' and 'Biscuit' was often heard by marching columns of soldiers from French and Belgian children keen to supplement their own diet. One reason for this was that both these staples of rations were regarded as being boring, the tins were heavy, especially for troops on the march, and could provide too much protein. One result of this was the all-too-frequent outbreaks of boils mentioned in many soldiers' memoirs. In addition to discarding the unwanted food items, British soldiers could supplement their rations, both with food from home and with privately purchased items intended to add flavour and variety to the issued food. This explains the profusion of food containers for mustard, pickles and sweets found in virtually every position occupied by British troops. It would be easy to regard these artefacts as being evidence of officers supplementing their rations, which they could well be as they received the same basic ration as the men, but the wide distribution and amounts of material suggest 'other ranks' rubbish. It is no coincidence that modern soldiers who have the advantage of boil-in-the-bag rations in assorted varieties still take curry powder, tabasco sauce and other flavourings and spices with them both when they are on exercise and when they are sent into action.

A good deal of a soldier's time out of the line was occupied by the search for food and drink. Even very close to the front line bars and estaminets were open where 'oeufs et frites' (egg and chips) were bought, accompanied by 'vin blanc' and beer. It can be argued that the term 'plonk' for cheap wine is a corruption of 'vin blanc', the staple ingredient of many evenings spent by soldiers of the BEF. The army also provided

An embossed Lea & Perrin's Worcester Sauce bottle found at Vimy Ridge. The sauce was a vital ingredient in any good corned-beef hash, even today. (*DRK*)

official canteens where tea and buns could be bought, and beer when it was available; these were supplemented by canteens run by charitable organisations, but often the dry (non-alcoholic) and morally improving tone of these establishments meant that soldiers preferred the easier ways of the local estaminets. R.A. Lloyd, a soldier in the Life Guards, described in his memoirs his time running the canteen for his cavalry brigade on the Somme. Armed with a GS wagon, a bell tent and a float from the brigade major, he stocked his tent 'shop' with 'cigarettes, bottled beer, cake, chocolate, and tobacco' and was able to sell out his complete stock daily for the three weeks he ran the concern.[9]

French soldiers tended to be issued with a greater percentage of fresh meat rather than tinned food. This was provided together with bread, vegetables, salted fish and some corned-beef referred to as 'Singe' or monkey. Each soldier received wine 'pinard' as a ration and this was increased as the war went on from a quarter to half a litre per day, although the soldiers still felt that it was insufficient. Like their British allies, French soldiers suffered from a lack of variety and they both scrounged and stole to address this problem. Canteens were established to provide chocolate and cigarettes, and tobacco was usually available to supplement the 100 grams provided weekly as a ration.[10]

If any soldiers had real reason to complain about their rations it was the Germans. Although the ration scale was quite generous at the outbreak of war, and included three-quarters of a kilo of bread (26 ounces), a third of a kilo of fresh meat, vegetables, tobacco and alcohol, wartime shortages meant that these rations were cut back rapidly. The meat ration was reduced progressively and from June 1916 there was one meatless day per week. The quality issued was also reduced and an even lower ration scale was introduced for troops not serving at the front. Increasingly 'Ersatz' or 'replacement' foods were issued, and coffee bulked out with acorns and adulterated flour became a feature of all German rations. Sadly the quality was such that 'Ersatz' came to mean sub-standard or poor, with dramatic effects on troop morale and efficiency.

One of the reasons for these reductions in rations was to ensure that selected front-line units such as 'storm troops' could receive a higher ration scale while other troops received less. However, the German military propaganda suggested that the Allies were suffering equal hardships and were on the verge of defeat. The success of the German offensive in the spring of 1918 disproved this lie as German units encountered well-stocked British depots stuffed with foods and stores they had not seen for years. The result was problems with large-scale looting, an orgy of drinking and mass indiscipline. Once the Allies went on the offensive in August 1918, over a million German soldiers deserted, most of them because they were desperate to try to feed their starving families back home, or to escape the failing military machine in which rations were largely unobtainable.

The archaeological consequences of all this eating are that every trench excavation is characterised by the discovery of huge amounts of food waste. In the case of the British army that means tins. Rusting empty tins are everywhere on the Western Front. They range from small but distinctive corned-beef tins, which have changed very little over time and are recognisable by their tapering rectangular shape, through to large 10lb (4.5kg) jam tins. The circular tins used for 'Maconochie Bros' meat and vegetable stew are also easily identified as they were very wide and shallow, being intended to fit inside a standard soldier's mess tin. The British army relied on tins as a form of packaging for almost every conceivable product, including meat, butter, cheese, jam, cigarettes, biscuits, milk (condensed) and chocolate.

And it's not just empty tins we find during excavation; full tins of corned-beef have been encountered on several occasions. Unfortunately the preservative qualities of the tin do not generally stand the test of time and the smell of the contents after ninety years is pungent to say the least. This raises another important point. Much of this refuse was simply thrown over the parapet into no-man's-land, or behind the trench, and the problems with flies and rats in the line are as much attributable to this kind of waste as to the more iconic unburied dead.

One more organised attempt at rubbish disposal was excavated in Thiepval Wood. Adjacent to one of the communication trenches a shell hole was uncovered containing a large pile of discarded tins, surrounded by wood ash and bearing significant evidence of burning. It seems someone had cleared up and started a bonfire of rubbish. That this took place during the war was apparent from the fact that parapet material thrown up in the improvement of the trench lay on top sealing over the burnt debris. Some unusual finds within this debris were the remains of several British ration biscuits. While such items would usually rot and disintegrate relatively quickly, these had been carbonised by the fire and preserved as a result.

The French, in contrast to the tinned supplies used by the British, issued much larger quantities both of fresh vegetables and of freshly butchered meat on the bone. This may reflect the fact that they were on home soil and thus nearer to their bases of supply, while much of the British food supply came from as far away as Argentina or North America. As a result positions occupied by French troops are often identifiable by significant deposits of discarded butchered animal bone. It is necessary for the excavator to become rapidly familiar with the skeletal differences between cows, sheep and humans in order to prevent false alarms.

Just because a collection of bones is found in the same shell hole as a set of discarded equipment it does not mean they aren't simply the leftovers of a lamb stew. Soldiers are creatures of habit and rapidly become accustomed to their regular diet, thus where the two nations were fighting together and received each other's rations complaints would be mutual, the French complaining of a lack of vegetables and the British bemoaning the lack of meat.

The greater problem for an individual soldier was not the supply of food but how to cook it. Any fires in the line would

A British ration biscuit, found in Thiepval Wood. It had been discarded in a shell-hole and was preserved after being carbonised by a subsequent fire. (*DRK*)

give their position away through smoke by day and light by night and thus attract shelling. As a result, any form of fire was severely restricted. Fuel was also a problem as this, along with everything else, would have to be brought forward by carrying parties and it was rarely high on the list of priorities. Fortunate troops might find themselves with a charcoal brazier, which could be persuaded to burn relatively smokelessly. Other troops became adept at heating tins of stew smokelessly or mess-tins of tea on shavings carefully whittled from a piece of waste wood or strips torn from a sandbag and helped along by a dribble of candle wax. Where the personal effects of soldiers have been excavated (associated with the dead as described in a later chapter) these often include candle ends, probably used not only for light but also for cooking.

Attempts were made to provide troops in the line with properly cooked hot food. Each company of the British army had a field kitchen capable of producing stews and hot drinks, but there were limits as to how close to the front these facilities could be brought. At first use was made of 'hay-boxes', large boxes filled with hay or straw to insulate an internal container or 'dixie' of food. As the war progressed purpose-designed insulated vessels were introduced. In the early part of the war this was one area where the Germans were ahead and their insulated food containers were much prized by both sides. The lid of one of these containers was uncovered at Thiepval, complete with the steam valve on the top. Sadly it seems that this was the exception rather than the rule, as the history of the 1/4th Duke of Wellington's Regiment, who occupied the wood in July and August 1916, records: 'There were no facilities for cooking, and so all food had to be sent up cooked from the transport lines. For six weeks no one had a decently prepared dinner.'[11]

Besides being invariably cold, the diet was extremely monotonous. One of the more interesting aspects of the excavation of Great War food refuse is the wide variety of condiment containers uncovered. Some of this was issued (mustard was on the ration) but the vast majority was privately purchased or received in parcels from home. Bottles of various types of sauce proliferate, often with the names of brands still common today embossed on the glass, or with fragmentary paper labels still surviving. Brown sauce, 'HP' sauce and 'Daddies' seem to have been very popular, along with Keiller's marmalades, identifiable by their distinctive printed white ceramic jars. (As an aside, Keiller went on after the war to spend some of the fortune he made by supplying the BEF with marmalade, on archaeology, funding work at Avebury stone circle as well as at other prehistoric sites.)

A tin of 'German' Camembert cheese found in the Hohenzollern Redoubt position at Loos. The words 'Deutschland' and 'Germany' are both apparent. (*UCL*)

Many of these products, far from having more utilitarian markings and packaging for dispatch to the front, used the fact that they were being supplied to the troops as a marketing tool and elaborate labels replete with patriotic messages are common, often incorporating the flags of the belligerent nations. One striking example excavated at the Hohenzollern Redoubt was a tin of Camembert cheese prominently marked 'Made in Germany' lest the Kaiser's men felt they were being offered 'enemy' cheese. It is easy to think of the Great War in the monochrome of the photography of the period, or as a vista of grey and khaki, but much harder to insert such vivid and brightly decorated food packaging into such an image.

COMFORTS

Food additives weren't the only items received in parcels from home. The postal service from the UK to the Western Front was fast and reliable, as was the equivalent service on the German side of the line. Letters and parcels generally reached their destinations within a few days, probably more quickly than an equivalent package would be delivered today. The army, knowing the importance of post to morale, also ensured that most parcels did make it to their intended recipients, thus family members could be confident that what they sent would arrive, and in a reasonably short time. The result of this was an enormous variety in the products posted, and various products were advertised on the home market which could be sent to 'your man in France' (some more practical than others).

The result of this is that every soldier would have in addition to his regulation kit and equipment an assortment of personal items. It is these which provide some of the most poignant of the artefacts found during excavation, leading as they do not to the khaki or field-grey soldier but to the individual inside the uniform. Sweets and chocolate were common, and tins for both have been uncovered, including toffee from

Soldiers of various units assembled outside a temporary field post office, indicated by the flag in the rear of the picture. One hopes no fragile parcels lay in the mail sacks being used as seats in the foreground. (*ASR*)

Harrogate, and chocolate described as 'A gift to his Majesty's forces from the Colonies of Grenada, St Lucia and St Kitts', the tin emblazoned with the heraldic crests of the colonies in question.

Tobacco was also ubiquitous, although here the archaeologist encounters one of the problems of varied preservation. While a glass 'HP' sauce bottle will survive in the soil indefinitely, a cardboard cigarette packet will not, and while these were also shipped in distinctive tins, a few of which have been found, many more must have been smoked than are represented by these containers. It is one of the features of Great War archaeology that the wealth of supporting documentary evidence allows the excavated data to be compared with the historical record, and such potential distortions of the evidence identified, unlike in earlier periods where this check is not available.

Surprisingly frequent finds are tobacco pipe components. Often the mouthpieces, carved from bone or other durable materials, survive, complete with the owner's teeth-marks around the end. In the German trenches at Serre several pipe-bowls were found, made in the continental style from ceramic material and decorated with elaborate moulded designs. Photographs of German troops often depict men sporting these types of pipe but whether the pipe was more common in the German army than among the cigarette-obsessed Tommies is unknown. On rare occasions of particularly good preservative conditions tobacco itself has been uncovered. One of the German casualties excavated at Serre (described in a later chapter) had a twist of newspaper in his pocket containing what appeared to be loose tobacco.

The other comfort to which soldiers throughout history have been addicted is of course alcohol, and the soldiers of the Great War were no exception. In the British army rum was part of the daily ration issue when on campaign and was often distributed in the cream and brown ceramic 'rum jars' that have become iconic collectors' items. These jars, in varying states of completeness, are a common find during excavation, but their function was more varied than is often assumed. An 'SRD' (Service Ration Depot) jar was often to be found full of lime juice or other liquids rather than rum, to the disappointment of many a Tommy. British officers also drank whisky in significant quantities, but wine acquired privately was also not uncommon in the trenches, and wine or even champagne bottles frequently appear in excavations. Bottles for non-alcoholic drinks also occur commonly, for cordials of various kinds and not uncommonly water. Perrier bottles in the distinctive shape they retain today have also been found.

In the French army the ration drink was wine, issued at a rate of a 'quart' or quarter-litre per day. The French soldier's drinking cup, a distinctive oval conical vessel, was designed to hold exactly this amount, and such cups have been recovered during excavation. German soldiers received spirits and beer, although this was more usually when they were not in the line. Unlike British soldiers, Germans were used to drinking water with their food and at the start of the war the German army took over a large number of bottling plants in the occupied zone and ration water frequently arrived in German positions in wine bottles. When the resultant empties were found in occupied German positions they suggested to the incredulous Allied troops high living and near permanent drunkenness among the German garrison.

HYGIENE AND CLEANLINESS

After eating and drinking the next preoccupation of the soldier in the trenches was trying to stay clean and healthy, a task which, given the frequently filthy conditions and the lack of water, could present a

A tube of privately purchased French toothpaste with a pink paper label bearing the words 'Beaute de Dents'. It was found in Thiepval Wood and provides clear evidence that the soldiers cared about their (in this case oral) hygiene. (*DRK*)

significant challenge. While most armies expected men to grow moustaches (the British *King's Regulations* made them compulsory at least at the beginning of the war), shaving of the remainder of the face was expected regularly. Thus shaving apparatus of all kinds frequently appears during excavation. Ceramic handles of several shaving brushes have been found, including one at Auchonvillers proudly marked by the manufacturer 'Guaranteed free from Anthrax' – hardly a risk one would associate with shaving today. Another brush, found in Thiepval Wood, consisted of a plated cylindrical tin which when opened proved to have a brush inside which could be removed and slotted on to the end of the tin to provide a handle. Associated with it were a cut-throat razor and part of a ceramic shaving-soap dish, providing the complete set, although whether these had been originally one man's set or whether the finds were coincidental will never be known.

Toothbrushes were also a standard issue item and a number of these have been recovered, often with the handle snapped off just behind the head. The design makes this a natural weak point of the brush. They may have been deliberately snapped at this point to make them more convenient to slip into a pocket, but it is more likely that this was the point at which they broke in use, and the ones discovered in excavation are those which broke and were discarded into the bottom of the trench. Thiepval Wood also produced a small tube of privately purchased French toothpaste, the printed label of which was still legible and bore the inscription 'Beaute de Dents' on a rather incongruous pink background. Hair combs have also been uncovered, and in the case of one of the German casualties excavated at Serre (discussed later) the comb was accompanied by a small fragment of mirror and a nail cleaner, suggesting a man more than usually concerned to maintain his appearance. It is details such as these which reveal the character of the individual soldier and provide a glimpse of the man behind the uniform.

A particularly satisfying find made at Thiepval in 2007 was a rolled-up gas cape containing a complete set of personal cleaning kit. The set

Detail of the shaving soap from Thiepval. The words 'Finlay's Shaving Soap, Est. 1798, Belfast Ireland' are all clearly readable. Perhaps this was the property of an Ulster Division soldier. (*DRK*)

An assemblage of personal items from Thiepval Wood: (*top*) spoon; (*middle*): shaving brush, 'housewife' with thimble, buttons and thread, comb, SMLE oil bottle, shaving soap; (*bottom*) razor (and modern ruler for scale). (*DRK*)

comprised a comb, a cut throat razor, a shaving brush, shaving soap, a spoon and a 'housewife' containing a thimble, spare shirt buttons and a shank of darning wool. There was also an oil bottle from an SMLE rifle and a bundle of paper. The shaving soap container was marked on its base 'Finlay's Shaving Soap, Est. 1798 Belfast, Ireland', which offers a tempting link to the soldiers of the 36th (Ulster) Division who occupied the wood before and during the opening fighting of the Somme battles in 1916.

The bundle of paper was examined, and some of the pages carefully prised apart. The condition of the bundle was very poor and only a few words could be made out, but these included frequent religious references and what appeared to be hymns. A date from 1915 was also apparent. It is likely that the paper was part of a religious pamphlet or tract. However, this does not imply that the soldier who carried it was particularly religious; in fact, the presence of the paper screwed up in his washing kit implies an altogether less godly function for the tract – as toilet paper. Toilet roll was not generally supplied to the troops at the front, indeed it was a rare luxury in civilian life. Instead people simply recycled whatever paper was to hand, old newspapers being a common resource, so each soldier would keep an eye out for any paper he could stuff into his pocket for later use.

This brings us to the often neglected question of bodily functions and human waste. Large numbers of men inevitably produced large amounts of waste, and the risk to health if not properly policed was significant. The discovery of a trench latrine in an old mortar pit at Beaumont Hamel has been discussed in an earlier chapter, but such features must have been common in all parts of the front, varying in their degree of comfort and sophistication from a purpose-built dug-out to a simple shelf in the trench. In the BEF at least, latrines were identified both at the time and archaeologically by the distinctive issue latrine bucket. This was oval in shape and about 2 feet (60 centimetres) long with slightly conical sides and a handle at each end. In addition to the one found *in situ* at Beaumont Hamel, other examples have been uncovered at Auchonvillers and in Thiepval Wood. Originally these would have been fitted with a canvas cover, and when full were emptied by specially appointed sanitary orderlies, under the command of a corporal. These men were naturally the butt of a good deal of humour, and the job was often given to men whose other military skills might have been lacking; however, as with all activities in the trenches, the job had its benefits. Chief among these was that a sanitary man might carry on his work in the safety of the trench while his comrades were out manning listening-posts in no-man's-land or performing some other similarly hazardous task. A curious postscript to this is that recently the authors passed an up-market florist in Chelsea, and saw in the window, marked for sale as planters, about twenty army latrine buckets. Sadly the shop was shut so there was no chance to discover whether the vendors were aware of what they were selling, and we missed the chance to add a couple to our collections. Great War artefacts can end up in some unexpected places!

At Auchonvillers one feature of the trench that proved exceptionally valuable was a sump dug to intercept rain water from a gully which had been cut into the side of the trench. The gully was just at the edge of the brick floor and was only a few inches deep, but was clearly cut with a General Service (GS) shovel. Whether through rain flow or simple luck (for the archaeologists, at least) numerous objects had been propelled into the sump and a mass of small artefacts was recovered. These included parts of a watch and a complete harmonica, one of the iconic objects associated with the Great War soldier. One advantage of this low-lying sump was that the moisture helped to preserve a variety of small objects from the British occupation of 1915 to 1918. A similar, but deeper, sump was also found during the work in Thiepval Wood. In the base of this pit four postholes were visible as cuts in the chalk, probably designed to carry a frame supporting a trench-board over this feature. The sump was also placed directly in front of a dug-out entrance so as to prevent water flowing into the entrance. It is noteworthy that the sump at Auchonvillers was placed in front of the probable second entrance to the cellar.

PERSONAL ITEMS

The various excavations have also produced a wealth of other personal items, including pens and pencils, harmonicas found at Auchonvillers and Serre, pocket change of various nationalities, penknives and cutlery. A copper alloy finger ring was also found in the lower fill of the German front-line trench at Serre. This caused some excitement as it would have been a personal item of some significance (although of little monetary value) to its owner. Sadly when it was examined in detail in the conservation laboratory it was found to be unmarked, so the story behind its loss will never be known.

Another find which caused some excitement was a spoon recovered from a communication trench in Thiepval Wood. A spoon in itself is not

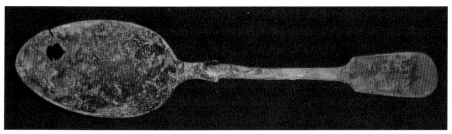

This spoon found in Thiepval Wood has an identifying number at one end and a bullet hole at the other. Research continues to find the fate of the owner of this item. (*DRK*)

a particularly unusual find, but on this occasion added interest was created by a bullet hole through the bowl of the spoon, and a stamped inscription reading 'WRR 19982' on the handle. Was it possible that the spoon had been carried by a soldier wounded or indeed killed by the bullet, and that the number might identify him? A tour group was visiting the wood at the time of this discovery and a number of people took photos of the inscription. Within 48 hours the internet chat-rooms were alive with possible identities for the owner of this cutlery, but life is never that simple. It is possible that 'WRR' refers to the West Riding Regiment, an informal title applied to battalions of the Duke of Wellington's Regiment, who served in the wood as part of the 49th (West Riding) Division. However, it may also be the man's initials. So far, searches in the National Archives by team members specialising in this kind of research have failed to produce a firm identity, but work continues.

What is notable is the excitement the find caused, and the efforts by members of the public to assist with the identification. Unfortunately it is easy to be over-enthusiastic about these things and while names may circulate on the web none has yet reached the required standard of proof. Coincidences between excavated finds and stories contained in documentary sources are commonplace on the Western Front, and it is easy to jump to the conclusion that particular items can be linked to particular events. It is the job of the archaeologist to remain sceptical on these occasions and to demand that the burden of proof remain as high as possible, otherwise we would be awash with poorly provenanced items, much as the Middle Ages were awash with the bones of saints and fragments of the True Cross.

Several watches, or parts of watches, have also been recovered. Part of one was recovered from the second-line trench at Beaumont Hamel. Such finds have additional significance in locations like this as time was such a key component of great offensives such as that on the Somme. Each stage of the assault was timed to the second in order to coordinate different parts of the attack, and to ensure artillery support fell in the right place at the right time, so having a good watch, particularly for officers, was thus literally a matter of life and death.

One watch in particular led the team on a fascinating path of research, but it also showed how it is possible to be led astray by coincidence. During the excavations at Forward Cottage near Ypres a wristwatch was uncovered; it was broken, and wrapped in newspaper. Wristwatches are one of the many modern inventions that have their origins in the Great War. Officers found that consulting a pocket watch kept in an inside pocket of a tunic was awkward, and so began to wear their watches around a wrist. Initially these were standard pocket watches, fitted into a specially designed strap with a case on it, but later purpose-built wristwatches became available. The watch found at Ypres was returned to the laboratory in London and examined. It was found to be an Ingersoll of American manufacture, but when the strap was cleaned it was found to have the word 'ENGLAND' stamped on it. Why would an American watch bear that inscription? Examination of the Commonwealth War Graves Commission records showed that a Lieutenant John England had served with the 4/5th Black Watch in the precise area where the excavation had taken place, and had been killed leading his men into battle on the first day of the third battle of Ypres, 31 July 1917. His remains were never found and he is remembered among the missing listed on the Menin Gate. To find a man of that name killed in the precise vicinity of the site seemed to be more than a coincidence, so could it be his watch?

After further cleaning of the watch strap the words 'MADE IN' could also be discerned, indicating that the inscription was not a name, but simply a manufacturer's stamp on a strap that had been acquired separately from the watch itself. Thus no connection could be made between the watch and the man. An eerie postscript was added to the story, however, when John England's service record was examined at the National Archives by one of the team's researchers. It was found to contain a letter from his father, who had written to the War Office to complain that after his son's death not all his personal effects had been returned. One of the missing items listed was a watch.

Chapter 4

Fighting in the Trenches

DEATH'S MEN

Up to this point this book has mostly been concerned with the soldiers' daily life, their struggle against the elements and their often cold, wet and miserable existence in the trench system. However, one should never forget the primary reason why they were there. The purpose of the BEF and all the men in it, as well as their French allies, was to eject the Germans from the occupied territories of France and Belgium. In short, there was a war on, and killing the enemy, while it may not have occupied the soldier's attention all the time, was ultimately his primary purpose.

Paradoxically, it is this most fundamental part of the soldier's job, and his experience, that is furthest from our own lives. While all of us can imagine being cold, wet or hungry, most of us are fortunate enough to have had no experience of fearing for our lives, and those of our friends, while simultaneously preparing to kill and wound others. In that sense then, the one thing that lay at the centre of the experience of a Great War soldier is the one thing we find it hardest to understand. Nor was this fear of death or injury focused on a single place or time, or based on one particular source of danger. Death could come at random behind the lines from a single isolated shell, or be concentrated in the visceral, almost prehistoric, hand-to-hand struggle for a section of trench during a raid or a larger offensive. Similarly, the tools at a soldier's disposal for killing his enemy, and in turn the same weapons which presented a threat to him, varied from the very large, such as siege artillery pieces which offered their gunners the chance to inflict impersonal and often unseen casualties on the enemy at a distance, down to the grenade and the bayonet, vital in close-up killing.

All of these aspects of combat are represented to some extent by archaeological remains, and the discovery of weapons and the equipment used in fighting, or in the case of artillery its effects on men and equipment, forms a powerful part of the picture of the war created by excavation. Moreover, the appropriateness and effectiveness of some weapons, in particular artillery, have been much debated since the war. Excavations examining in close detail the effectiveness of these weapons can shed an interesting new light on these debates. In this chapter the focus will be on combat and the tools used for it, but also it is hoped to go beyond the technology and gain some insight, however small, into what the experience of combat was like for the individual soldier.

ARTILLERY

We start with the big stuff. While the machine-gun has an iconic reputation as a killer of men during the Great War, it was the artillery which presented the greatest omnipresent daily threat to the soldiers, and was also often the biggest killer during offensive operations. Unless a man was involved in a rare major attack or daylight trench raid, his chances of being hit by bullets were low. While in the trenches, unless he was seen by a sniper during the day or caught by machine-gun fire or rifles out on patrol or in a wiring party in no-man's-land, the most lethal

Bombardment of La Boiselle, Somme, June 1916. A large-calibre British High Explosive shell has burst, creating the large column of black smoke, while smaller shrapnel shell air-bursts are also visible. (*Imperial War Museum: Q23*)

weapon was artillery. Whether it was shrapnel bursting overhead or high explosive shells landing in the trenches, it was the guns that killed and wounded the majority of men. Even on the first day of the battle of the Somme it has been estimated that as many as half the British casualties were caused by artillery as they toiled across no-man's-land or cowered in captured German trenches.

Up until 1916 it was a common misconception among commanders on both sides that artillery could be used to destroy trenches on a large scale and kill the men in them. The plan for 1 July 1916 in particular was based on the idea that sufficient shelling would kill all the Germans in the enemy front-line trenches and then the British and French forces would be able simply to walk over and occupy these positions. Tragically this proved not to be the case. A similar misunderstanding has developed since the war concerning the effect of the German defensive artillery. The popular image of the Somme is of the advancing troops being mown down by machine-guns. While there is no doubt that this happened, equal or greater numbers of men were killed and wounded by the German counter-bombardment of the areas of no-man's-land across

An 18-pdr crew hard at work in the summer heat during the Somme battle. Ready rounds are visible on the left, fired cases on the right. The lip of the shallow rectangular excavation of the 'gun pit' is also apparent in front of the right-hand wheel. (*Imperial War Museum: Q4065*)

which the attackers were advancing. Thus it was the man in the open, in this case the attacker, who was most vulnerable to artillery, rather than the man in the trench.

Even when a major attack was not in progress it was paradoxically not the men in the front line who had most to fear from artillery. Shells were dropped on the front-line trenches and casualties were inflicted there, but the preferred targets of artillery spotters were those areas behind the line which men and equipment had to cross but which were less well protected. With much of the battlefield badly damaged, road junctions, communication trenches and other key points which formed bottlenecks for movement in and out of the trenches became key targets. Even if the gunners could not see these positions directly, their positions could be worked out from maps and aerial photographs, and rounds fired speculatively at times of day when traffic was likely to be heavy, such as at mealtimes or when units were being relieved in the line.

Close examination of trench maps of the period shows that in many cases those rear locations which provided good artillery targets were

A shell crater in Thiepval Wood under excavation in front of the television cameras. One team member on the right seems less than gripped by Alex's explanations! (*DRK*)

carefully recorded and pre-registered. Rather than using long-winded grid coordinates, each position was given a simple code number so that guns could be quickly brought to bear on that location simply by passing on the relevant location code. The evidence of this can be seen archaeologically. As part of the work in Thiepval Wood a topographic survey was carried out, and all of the visible shell holes were plotted. This plan showed a clear concentration of shell holes at the junction of the front-line trench with a communication trench known as 'Creepy Street' (a particularly idiosyncratic name). The spot had obviously been selected as a bottleneck through which many men would have to pass, and had been targeted accordingly.

An interesting result of the surveying of the shell holes in Thiepval Wood, and the excavation of one of them, was the speculation that arose concerning the origins of the shell which had created the crater itself.

A high-angle shell from a howitzer or large gun creates a roughly circular shell crater. However, a field gun, assuming it is firing a high explosive shell rather than shrapnel, will create a more oval crater aligned with the flight path of the shell. One such oval crater was identified in the wood. It was a simple job to take a compass bearing along the long axis of the crater and to plot this line on a trench map. Perhaps not surprisingly, but none the less to the archaeologists' satisfaction, the line led directly to an area behind the German lines known as 'Battery Valley', so called because a number of German artillery positions lay there. Further, in the course of excavating the crater a German fuse was uncovered. Our EOD expert identified it as a type of fuse used on shells fired from a particular obsolete pattern of German field gun. Very few of these guns were deployed on the Somme battlefield, and only one or two of them made it to 'Battery Valley' in particular. A tempting and rather tantalising theory was developed as a result, that we might be able to identify the very piece, and the corresponding German artillery unit, that had fired the shell. Of course, this relied on a series of highly questionable bits of data being strung together to produce what could only be a matter of speculation rather than hard fact, but it shows just how far it is possible to go when combining documentary and archaeological evidence together. Of course, it also gave some of the team members an opportunity to show off their knowledge of obsolete German field guns.

As was alluded to earlier, one of the most famous and controversial artillery bombardments of the war was that prior to the attack on the Somme on 1 July 1916. More than 1,000 field guns and 450 heavy guns fired one and a half million shells at the German defenders and their defences. Perhaps the most controversial aspect of this bombardment was the use of large numbers of 18-pdr (field gun) shrapnel shells to cut the German barbed wire. Although this technique was effective in theory, it required very precise timing of the shell fuses, and on many parts of the front it turned out not to be up to the job, despite the vast quantity of shells fired. The problem was that although the British army had a greatly improved stock of artillery shells, compared to the desperate shortage of 1915, the majority of the supply for field guns continued to be shrapnel rather than high explosive. In any case the fuses fitted to British high explosive shells at that time functioned so slowly that the explosion would only be triggered after the shell had buried itself in the ground. This would greatly reduce the effectiveness of such shells against a barbed wire entanglement. Thus there was really no choice but to use shrapnel.

Clear evidence of this bombardment was uncovered during the excavations at Serre. A long thin excavation area was dug across the line of the German main line of defence, a trench known as the *Bayern Graben*. Numerous components of shrapnel shells were found at that site. A shrapnel shell is designed to explode in the air above its target, rather like a large flying shotgun. When it has done so, unlike a high explosive shell its component parts remain surprisingly intact. The casing of the shell is thickened and designed not to fragment when the shell bursts; rather it stays in one piece working as the 'barrel' of the shotgun. Inside are a large number of individual shrapnel balls, a piston-like ring which forces the balls out of the case, and a long 'flash-tube' connecting the fuse at the front of the shell to the explosive charge at the base. All of these parts, along with the fuse itself, fly off to inflict damage on the enemy, or in this case the barbed wire. In turn, all of these pieces can survive to be recovered by excavation. In an area of about 100 square metres no fewer than forty-one fuse fragments were recovered, along with eleven base-plates and thirteen flash-tube parts. Seven shell casings were also recovered. No doubt detailed analysis of all these components would allow a calculation of how many individual shells they actually represent. The team did not attempt this, but it is clear that these parts reflect a large number of shells falling on a relatively small area – graphic evidence of the intensity of the bombardment.

The difficulty of using shrapnel shells in this context was also illustrated. We found several shells that had buried themselves in the clay before exploding. The fuse and all the shrapnel balls from within the shell were found forced into the clay only a few centimetres out from the mouth of the casing. Clearly this would have had little effect on the surrounding barbed wire. As the fuse was based on a time delay not on impact, any errors in the setting of this time would render the shell ineffective. Only in 1917 was the so-called No. 106 'instantaneous' fuse introduced. This fuse was designed to explode the shell extremely quickly, such that if it struck barbed wire it would burst immediately without burying itself in the ground. This allowed high explosive shells to be used very effectively against barbed wire. It was at around the same time that planners started to appreciate that a bombardment on a trench system did not in fact kill many of the occupants; it merely forced them underground while the bombardment persisted. As soon as the shelling finished it became a race between the attackers crossing no-man's-land, and the defenders trying to get out of their dug-outs and install their machine-guns to prevent them doing so. A new strategy was developed relying only on a very short 'hurricane' bombardment to keep the enemies' heads down while the attack itself took place, rather than wasting weeks in advance trying to kill them all with high explosive. The battle of Cambrai in November 1917 is an example of an offensive where the bombardment began only at the same time as the infantry attack, thus allowing a significant degree of surprise to be maintained.

Thus far we have concentrated on the effects of artillery on infantry and trenches. In fact, at least as much time, if not more, in a gunner's life was spent in his private battle with the enemy's artillery. Given the damage that a defensive barrage could do to attacking troops in the open it was vital in any offensive to neutralise the opponent's artillery. As soon as a gun fired it risked giving away its position to the enemy. It would then attract counter-battery fire on to its own position. Throughout the war a constant game of cat-and-mouse was played between the artillery forces of both sides trying to locate all the enemy's guns and in turn hide their own. It also made the artilleryman's job much more dangerous than it might at first sight appear, as every time his gun fired he risked retaliatory shelling. By the end of the war the techniques for detecting enemy gun positions were highly sophisticated. 'Flash-spotting', for example, used bearings taken by several observers on the flash of a gun firing, while 'sound-ranging' used an array of microphones to triangulate on the sound of the gun. As was discussed in an earlier chapter, it is probable that the concrete emplacement excavated by the team at La Signy Farm was in fact a flash-spotting post. The embrasure in the front of the post was much larger than would be required, for example, for a machine-gun, but the wide field of view it provided would have been ideal for flash-spotting.

So far the team has not investigated and excavated a large artillery position. Such features remain on the long list of Great War structures we have not yet had a chance to examine. Maybe in the future we will be able to dig one. However, we did find an unusual feature in Thiepval Wood which was interpreted as a field gun position. An area was excavated in a location which it was thought would reveal part of the front-line trench from 1916. Instead, a shallow rectangular pit was uncovered. In the floor of this pit was a sloping slot, deeper at its outer end than in the centre. This feature initially caused a good deal of puzzlement. The answer came when excavation was extended to a nearby section of trench. In the trench was a complete 18-pdr round, the brass propellant casing being complete with a fused shell still attached on the top. Close examination by our EOD expert revealed a striker mark on the percussion cap on the base of the case. Apparently it was a dud; having failed to fire it had been taken out of the gun and discarded. There was no reason why such a dud shell would be found anywhere except extremely close to the position of a gun. This explained the rectangular pit. Also the 18-pdr QF (Quick Firer) gun has only a single pole trail. In order to fire the gun at a high elevation it was common practice to dig a slot and lower the back of the trail, allowing a few degrees of extra elevation to the barrel. This was what the slot in the floor of the pit was for. Interpreting this feature would have been much more difficult had the shell not been found. As always, the context of the artefacts was key. As an aside to this story, this feature also demonstrated the dynamic character of the battlefield discussed in an early chapter. As with the mortar pit which became a latrine when the battle moved forward, it is extremely unlikely that a field gun would have been found in that location on 1 July 1916, but as the battle moved northwards in the autumn and winter of that year, the guns would naturally have had to be moved forward also, into positions which had formerly been in or even beyond the front line. (The possibility that the position was built during the fighting of 1918 also cannot be ruled out.)

MACHINE-GUNS

Machine-guns were a vital part of the arsenals of all the belligerent forces during the Great War. Both the British and the German armies relied on a similar basic type, the Maxim gun, which was developed in the late nineteenth century, although by the start of the war the British army was using a lighter, more refined version manufactured by Vickers. Initially these guns were issued at a rate of two per battalion, but this figure was to rise in the course of the war. Likewise, at the start of the war the guns were manned by crew members drawn from within the ranks of each battalion, but in 1915 the separate Machine Gun Corps (MGC) was formed, and the guns were concentrated in a machine-gun company allocated to each brigade. In the German army machine-guns remained under the control of individual regiments, but as each regiment had three battalions, equivalent to a British brigade, the effect was similar.

A distinctly battered Machine Gun Corps shoulder title recovered in Thiepval Wood. The bent letters 'MGC' are discernible. Questions about how it became so distorted and what happened to its owner immediately spring to mind. (*DRK*)

Unfortunately the team has not yet had the opportunity to excavate a purpose-built machine-gun position. On the two occasions when we thought we might have found a machine-gun position, the features turned out to be the flash-spotting post and the field gun emplacement discussed above. Nor has much evidence of these weapons been found among the backfill of trenches in general. Machine-guns were much too large and valuable to leave casually lying around, and even if damaged they would not have been discarded but salvaged for parts. The only direct evidence uncovered so far consists of a short length of broken Vickers tripod leg and an extremely distorted brass MGC shoulder title found near the front line in Thiepval Wood. On their own these two objects do not provide concrete evidence for anything, but they do evoke the possibility that they are the remains of a machine-gun and its crew, which took a direct hit from artillery. Certainly the Vickers machine-gun

An Australian infantry platoon in August 1918. Two Lewis gunners can be seen and at least five other men in the platoon are carrying the circular pouches containing the ammunition drums for the guns. (*Imperial War Museum: E (AUS) 2790*

leg will not simply break: only great external force would fracture one of these items. Machine-gun positions were certainly second only to artillery positions in receiving the attentions of enemy gunners.

One important development in the British army which the Germans were never able to match satisfactorily was the introduction of a light machine-gun used within infantry platoons. This was the famous Lewis gun adopted in late 1914; by the end of the war each British or Dominion platoon might have as many as four of these weapons. Indeed, the British general and tactician Ivor Maxse remarked that 'A platoon without a Lewis gun is not a platoon at all.' Again no evidence of these guns themselves has been uncovered during excavations. However, the ammunition was carried up, and supplied to the gun in circular metal drums. Examples of these have been found on several sites, including Serre and Thiepval Wood. The interesting taphonomic processes which occur during the corrosion of these objects have already been discussed in an earlier chapter. It is probable that Lewis gun drums are found more often in excavation because they were used in quite fluid fighting, rather than in static purpose-built positions, and thus more chance arose that the crew would abandon or lose drums in the course of fighting. Those at Thiepval Wood were found in the fill of a sap adjacent to the parapet of the front-line trench, and so it is possible that they were stored or placed on the parapet ready for use and subsequently became lost and buried. The discovery of items associated with Lewis guns has always been greeted with some excitement by the team, not least because the grandfather of one of the authors was a Lewis gunner. This is yet another example of how excavated objects from the war can have a special resonance for people because of their own individual connections with the conflict.

The Lewis gun drums found at Serre resonated with another personal story. Here a number of drums were found next to a barbed wire trench-block within the 'Heidenkopf' trench system. The team was investigating this area because of its associations with the poet Wilfred Owen during January 1917. Owen himself recorded in a letter to his mother the possible court-martial of an officer of the Highland Light Infantry (which had relieved Wilfred's own unit) for abandoning three Lewis guns when retreating from their part of the trench system.[12] Of course it is extremely unlikely that these drums are those abandoned by that officer. We do not even know the precise location of the event. However, it is surprising how often items come to light in excavation which echo stories available in documentary sources. It is extremely rare that archaeological discoveries can be tied directly to pre-existing literary material. To attempt to do so places the excavator in the same realm as American Christian fundamentalist archaeologists who dig in the Holy Land in the attempt to somehow 'prove' the Bible. It's not possible: archaeology simply does not work like that. None the less, to be able to show that similar events took place on the battlefield allows us to give more substance to the picture created in our imagination by the literature.

PERSONAL WEAPONS AND EQUIPMENT

In addition to the wide range of larger weapons provided for his support, the private soldier was also armed and equipped to fight as an individual in his own right. Items of soldiers' personal equipment form a large part of the total assemblage recovered from any site. Indeed, after shell fragments and food tins, small arms ammunition is probably the next commonest find on any site. Mention has been made in an earlier chapter of the practice of discarding ammunition rather than risking loading dirty bullets into a weapon. The result of this is that rifle rounds, both fired and unfired, turn up constantly on site, forming a sort of background noise in any excavation. The fact that both the nationality and the date of manufacture of these objects can easily be determined

Experimental archaeology: Andy Robertshaw compares excavated fragments of 1914 pattern equipment with a museum example donned by Belgian team member Janiek de Gryse. (*DRK*)

means that they provide a useful general guide to the date and nationality of the particular area of activity being investigated. This effect is comparable to the large amounts of pottery sherds that might be found on a Roman site, for example, which would be used in a similar way to provide general dating information.

Typically, each soldier was provided with a huge range of weapons and other equipment which he was expected to carry around. In addition, he was supplied with a set of leather or webbing belts and straps to carry it all. Individual items such as entrenching tools, water bottles, bayonets, ammunition and the like frequently turn up in excavation, but sometimes pieces of personal equipment – and, rarely, whole sets – are also found. The common English term for personal equipment is 'webbing', because the 1908 pattern of personal equipment in the British army was made from canvas webbing. However, this was relatively new and unusual. Prior to 1908 British personal equipment was made from leather, and French and German equipment continued to be made in that material. Indeed, due to a shortage of available canvas webbing in 1914, the British introduced a 'Pattern 1914' set of personal equipment which was also made of leather. Unlike the new Mills equipment which was made from cotton webbing and had to be woven on special looms by the Mills Equipment Company, any company that sewed horse harnesses and saddlery, shoes or even belts could make leather webbing. However, the army had

German belt equipment found at Bixschoote, seen here prior to cleaning. The belt and pouches are above, with a water bottle and entrenching tool holder to lower left. Lower right is a museum example of the pouches for comparison. (*DRK*)

switched from leather to webbing because it was more durable, more comfortable to wear and more versatile in terms of camouflage.

Due to the processes of decay over time, canvas webbing equipment rarely survives in the soil. However, the straps were connected together with a great many brass buckles and sliders, and the ends of the straps were prevented from fraying by brass strap-ends. All of these metal parts survive very well and are frequently encountered in excavation. Sometimes individual buckles are found on their own, but often buckles and strap-ends are found lying in relative positions which show that they were originally connected together by webbing that has since rotted away. Fortunately for the archaeologist, leather equipment survives much better in the soil, and the team has uncovered a number of more or less complete sets of both British 1914 pattern and German personal equipment. In particular a spectacularly preserved set of German equipment was found at Bixschoote in Belgium.

When the clay had been cleaned off, it was still possible to read the original manufacturer's name and date stamps on the leather. This revealed that it had been made in Hamburg. Written on it in ink was the letter R for Regiment, together with the number 8 and then either a 9 or a 3. We could not identify it beyond doubt, but it demonstrated that both stamped and written information can survive on leather in the right conditions.

The British 1914 pattern leather equipment was issued in particular to large numbers of the volunteer New Army troops who fought for the first time on the Somme. These units cursed its various failings, not least because it so clearly marked them out from the regulars and Territorials. In consequence, New Army soldiers were at great pains to acquire webbing equipment and discard the stigmatising 1914 sets. As a result, battlefield archaeology reveals a disproportionate amount of this leather equipment which was discarded by men who had found sets of the coveted webbing abandoned by the wounded or no longer required by the dead. A number of apparently complete sets of 1914 pattern equipment have been found in Thiepval Wood in particular. It is tempting to suggest that these were deliberately discarded when webbing equipment became available, but since the webbing equipment typically does not survive, it is impossible to say whether an equal or larger number of sets of webbing equipment was also lost or discarded in the wood. This is a good example of how differential preservation can perhaps lead to a misinterpretation of the evidence. Of course, soldiers in the trenches did not typically walk around burdened by their entire

An SMLE rifle found on the floor of the front-line trench in Thiepval Wood. The sling as well as parts of the wooden stock are visible. Why would an intact weapon be abandoned? (*DRK*)

equipment. As period photographs show, personal equipment was hung, draped and dumped all over the place in the trenches while the owners got on with other things. It is hardly surprising that a significant quantity of this material was not picked up again.

The other piece of kit which the great majority of front-line soldiers would have carried is of course the rifle. The rusted metal parts of rifles from all the major powers are a common sight on the Western Front, in 'rust and dust' museums in particular. However, they bear little resemblance to their original condition, with the wooden stock almost entirely rotted away and the formerly smooth and oiled metal parts brown with rust. Relatively few rifles have been found in excavation, possibly because the archaeologists have focused on sections of trench and other regularly occupied positions where it is unlikely that rifles, even if badly damaged, would have been left lying around. Moreover, salvage teams were given the task of collecting both serviceable and damaged weapons after each battle. Many of those found by farmers were probably lost in no-man's-land, in shell holes or in other places where they were unlikely to have been reclaimed. None the less the team did uncover one British SMLE rifle from the floor of the front-line trench in Thiepval Wood. This weapon was in excellent condition when uncovered. The bayonet was fixed and the wooden stock and leather sling survived remarkably intact. Unfortunately the wood had decayed to such an extent that it did not survive the lifting of the rifle, but it was possible to record it *in situ* in the trench. What is curious about this find is why an apparently intact rifle would be left lying on the floor of a trench rather than being recovered. Clearly it was not simply dropped by a sentry and forgotten, as might be the case with a smaller item. Something pretty dramatic must have been happening for soldiers to overlook the loss of a rifle. Sadly we will never know what particular dramas that rifle witnessed.

COMBAT – THE ATTACK

Once a soldier had been transported to the front, fed, clothed, equipped, armed and provided with a trench, he came to the 'heart of the matter': fighting the enemy. For the British and French at least this would sooner or later mean taking part in a major offensive. For the German soldier, unless he was involved in one of the relatively rare large-scale German attacks, such as at Verdun, his experience would be of waiting for the British or French to attack him. In between these large-scale offensives both sides kept up an active programme of raiding into the enemy's trenches. Naturally a multitude of specialists of all kinds, from gunners to signallers to tunnellers to cooks and storekeepers, were involved in a large offensive, but for the junior ranks of the infantry their task was a simple one: they had to get from their own trench into that of the enemy, and on arrival fight him for it. Local raiding differed in that often the approach to the enemy trench could be made more safely in secret, but the fighting in the enemy line was likely to be just as brutal, with the added danger of having to try to get back to your own line afterwards.

The iconic image of the British Tommy in the Great War struggling out of his trench so overburdened with equipment that he could barely walk, let alone run, and then having to advance towards uncut barbed wire in the face of massive machine-gun and artillery fire is firmly ingrained in the psyche of the nation. However, like many such myths this image requires closer examination. It is true that in the attack British soldiers were heavily burdened. In addition to their personal equipment discussed earlier, each man was issued with additional trench stores such as barbed wire, picks and shovels, extra ammunition, telephone cable, or a multitude of other items. It is an unfortunate fact of military life that without this heavy burden of extra equipment, capturing the enemy trench would have been pointless as the soldiers would have been unable to defend it. The German defenders, by contrast, were able to fight in relatively simple belt order carrying only ammunition and other immediate necessities, since they remained in their own trench with all the heavy equipment near at hand.

Although the soldiers had to carry all this extra stuff, the belief that it rendered them practically immobile is erroneous. Since the time of Julius Caesar it has been a fairly well established military principle that an individual soldier can move and fight effectively while carrying around 60–80lbs (30–40kg) of personal kit. This natural physical limit has defined the burden on British soldiers from Waterloo to the Somme, and indeed on to the streets of Iraq in the early twenty-first century, where the addition of modern ballistic body armour has added a significant extra weight to a soldier's kit. Despite this heavy load, most fit young soldiers are still able to run and fight reasonably effectively. Nor were very many soldiers in the Great War expected to go 'over the top' (or in the more typical parlance of the period, 'Hop the Bags') and walk towards the enemy in long lines, despite the widely held myth. In fact many plans of attack were much more sophisticated, including advances by short rushes supported by firepower, as well as other techniques. The historian Gary Sheffield examined the 1 July 1916 attack in particular, and found that of the 80 attacking battalions on that day only 12 advanced in the classic walking waves of popular imagination. The other 68, the vast majority, used a more subtle and effective means of crossing no-man's-land.

The site of the team's excavation at Thiepval Wood is justly famous for the exploits of the Ulster Division on 1 July. However, it often comes as a surprise to visitors to be shown the excavated entrance from the front-line trench into one of the saps which the division constructed across no-man's-land for their attack. The Ulstermen used these saps to creep out into no-man's-land, very close to the German wire, *before* the time of the offensive. At 7.30am their attack began not with a whistle but with a bugle, and with the men already deployed in no-man's-land no one went 'over the top' as such at all. It is also worth noting that the Ulster Division's attack was a complete success, with the men reaching the German third-line defensive system ahead of schedule, and before the bombardment of it was complete. Sadly the failure of the divisions on either side rendered the Ulstermen's position untenable and they had to withdraw. In this case the excavated archaeology, the front-line trench and sap, can be used to illustrate a version of events on 1 July quite different from that which the visitor might expect.

Once into the enemy trench serious close-up fighting could be expected. In this context the rifle became less important, except perhaps as a support for the bayonet, and the hand grenade or 'bomb' was supreme. In the British army the term bomb was ubiquitous, not least because the Grenadier Guards objected to the word grenadier being applied to any soldier outside their prestigious regiment. Hand grenades of a wide variety of types have been uncovered during excavation. Most common of course is the British No. 5 grenade or Mills bomb with its characteristic segmented casing. However, a wide range of other types has been found, including German 'stick', 'egg' and 'disc' grenades as well as French types and various sorts of rifle grenade. These items of course remain extremely dangerous today, and so are only handled and excavated by our trained EOD support staff. Even during the war grenades were considered a hazard, and were transported separately from the fuses. Only at the last minute before an attack would the detonator sets be added and the grenades issued. It was not uncommon for each man to be given several to carry into the attack, although he was not necessarily expected to use them himself – more often they were to be passed forward when required to be used by the specialist bombers

Some of the cache of No. 5 grenades ('Mills bombs') found in a communication trench in Thiepval Wood. Initially they were found in a jumbled pile but here have been laid out after being individually excavated by our EOD expert. (*DRK*)

within the section or platoon. In one trench in Thiepval Wood a cluster of over 100 grenades was uncovered; all were fused and ready to go. It is likely that they had been prepared for use and put in batches into sandbags which would then be carried forward to supply the bombers. For whatever reason these had been lost or discarded before use. In any event they provided our EOD officer with a morning's work to lift them safely, before work in that section of trench could be resumed. One of the most famous stories associated with Thiepval is that of Private McFadzean of the 14th Royal Irish Rifles, who was awarded a posthumous Victoria Cross for throwing himself bodily on to several grenades that were dropped while being issued to passing soldiers, thus saving many of his comrades from injury in the subsequent blast.

The trenches in the area of the 'Heidenkopf' at Serre were also fiercely contested, not least during the period when Wilfred Owen was present in January 1917. A number of unused German grenades were found in these trenches, as well as fragments of others which had exploded. In addition several 'knife-rests' were uncovered. These were metal frameworks to which barbed wire was attached. They could be used on the surface as part of a larger wire entanglement, but were also positioned on the parapet of trenches ready to be pulled down into the trench to create a block if the enemy managed to break in. It is possible that these items were simply thrown into the trench after the war during the clear-up, but the possibility also remains that they were *in situ*, where they had been dragged down to block the trench in the course of the fighting. Interestingly, the Lewis gun drums found during this excavation, discussed earlier, were uncovered immediately behind the 'knife-rest'. It is possible that they reflect the defence of the block by a Lewis gunner.

One of the results of this kind of fighting was that as the war progressed soldiers focused more and more on the bomb as the key weapon in individual fighting at the expense of the rifle. Indeed, by 1917 the British high command was becoming concerned about the falling standard of musketry among the troops, and pressed for it to be brought back up to standard. It is unlikely, however, that the conscripts of 1917 and 1918 would ever have reached the supreme standard of musketry of the pre-war BEF. The other concept which senior commanders constantly urged upon the junior ranks was the 'spirit of the bayonet'. Bloodthirsty training courses were established in an effort to instil in the common soldier a burning desire to stab his enemy. To what extent this was successful is highly questionable. In fact the 'spirit of the bayonet' is a bit of a misnomer. Despite the fact that all soldiers were issued with a bayonet primarily designed for injuring the enemy, this was possibly its least common use. Numerous bayonets, both broken and complete, have been found in excavation. However, this does not mean that the excavation areas were the scenes of brutal fighting. Bayonets were much more commonly used for everything from opening tins to splitting firewood and scraping mud off boots than for fighting. In fact, if troops expected to have to fight hand to hand, a variety of improvised weapons would be chosen in preference to a bayonet. These included home-made clubs, revolvers, sharpened spades and entrenching tools, knuckle-dusters, and purpose-made trench knives. The fearsome looking 'saw-back' on some German patterns of bayonet was probably not intended to inflict nastier wounds on the enemy; more likely, as its name suggests, it was intended to be used as a saw. No fewer than three bayonets were found during the excavation of a mortar pit at Thiepval, two of which were found driven up to the hilt into the walls of the pit. It is probable that rather than serving any warlike purpose these bayonets had been simply used as coat-pegs.

Soldiers of all nationalities have an amazing capacity to subvert the intended functions of the equipment issued to them and to turn items intended for dealing death to the enemy to domestic use, and *vice versa*. The archaeologist always has to bear this in mind when examining what appear at first sight to be instruments of war found during his excavations. At other times the evidence of the savagery of combat is unequivocal. However, this is more often apparent in the evidence of the consequences of weapon use, evidence of death and wounding, and of the remains of soldiers themselves, discussed in the next chapter, rather than simply by uncovering the weapons.

TECHNOLOGY

Another of the enduring themes of the Great War is the rapid integration into the arsenals of the belligerents of a wide range of new technology. The war is seen as 'technological' and 'twentieth century' in character in a way that no previous conflict had been. The new inventions that were introduced also serve as metaphors for describing the character of the war, and appear in many of the literary responses to it, from serious military history to poetry and the fiction dealing with the conflict. Machines are often seen in opposition to man, as if the war itself were one large machine intent on devouring its participants, or on the other hand as new and revolutionary developments which the generals planning the war failed to understand. In both cases the technology is deemed to have added a new and increased level of horror to the conflict. There is not space here to deal fully with these two lines of thought, and it is questionable whether any war is more or less ghastly than any other: the mass killing that occurred in a small space at Waterloo or Borodino is comparable in many respects to any of the battles of the Great War. The new technologies do, however, provide an interesting addition to the range of material encountered on site. The team has not yet been able to identify any components of aircraft in excavation, but we have been able to find objects associated with a vast range of other new-fangled devices, from telephones to tanks and mortars to mining machinery.

The trench mortar, of all the new weapons invented during the war, was possibly the one whose use became most widespread. The German army had mortars when the war began, although these had been developed to deal with the defences likely to be encountered when assaulting the forts that were a feature of both France and Belgium's frontiers and major cities. The British army, having planned for a war of movement, lacked both mortars and even hand grenades in any number when the war began. As a result, in answer to the German deployment of mortars in trench warfare, the British response was hesitant, but ultimately successful. The sappers and miners of the Meerut Division, part of the Indian Corps serving in Northern France and Belgium in mid-November 1914, manufactured the first 'British' mortars.[13] These first mortars, improvised from drain tubes and black powder, were rapidly phased out in favour of equally dangerous devices made from iron water pipes and jam tins, manufactured close behind the front lines in workshops by the First Army. By late 1915 two patterns were in use; these were manufactured in the United Kingdom and, if they did have some vices, they were at least more reliable. One was the 2-inch medium mortar or 'toffee apple' that remained in use from late 1915 until 1917. The other was the Stokes mortar. Wilfred Stokes' mortar had a 3-inch calibre barrel supported by bipod legs, and with an initial range of 430 yards and a high rate of fire it became the standard mortar for the British army. The pattern was so successful that 4-inch, 6-inch and other variants were developed that could fire gas and smoke ammunition.[14]

The first time the team encountered evidence of mortars was during the excavation of the latrine pit and former mortar position at Beaumont Hamel. However, because of its subsequent conversion into a latrine,

little evidence of the mortar itself was found, other than the sandbagged recess in the floor used to support the base-plate. A later investigation of a mortar pit in Thiepval Wood was more fruitful. This excavation was remarkable for the completeness of the range of artefacts uncovered and for the detailed 'story' which could be reconstructed from them.

The remains of a 2-inch 'Toffee apple' mortar *in situ* in the mortar pit excavated at Thiepval. The iron parts of the base are visible, along with a void where the timber has rotted away. Note also the sockets for the supporting timbers in the four corners of the pit. (*DRK*)

A 'Toffee apple'. The travelling plug is visible in the fuse socket on the top, along with the lettering '2" Trench How.r [Howitzer] V.S.M. [Vickers & Sons Maxim] 2/16 [February 1916]'. (*DRK*)

The feature was identified on the surface as a shallow depression in the ground approximately 5m long and 3m wide. After digging down for approximately a metre, the archaeologists uncovered several sheets of collapsed corrugated iron, along with the remains of several horizontal beams and the tops of four upright posts. These were the remains of the roof which covered the rearward part of the post. When these had been recorded and removed, a square pit was revealed, cut into the solid chalk to a depth of about 10 feet (2.5 metres). The sides of this pit were covered with expanded metal mesh, which had bowed inwards after collapsing to create an hour-glass shape within the pit. After a week of furious digging the floor of the pit was reached, and to our intense satisfaction the base-plate of a mortar was found still *in situ* set into the floor of the pit. At this point our week of digging was up and the pit had to be backfilled with sandbags full of earth and left over the winter. We eagerly returned the following spring, when the pit was fully excavated and revealed a remarkable assemblage of objects.

In the floor of the pit was the base-plate of a 2-inch ML trench howitzer, more commonly known as a 'toffee-apple mortar' from the shape of the bombs it fired. Further digging produced the elevating mechanism of the weapon, along with two of the bombs themselves. These mortars were fired using an adapted Lee-Enfield rifle breech, and a specially shaped blank .303 cartridge. A number of these cartridges were found on the floor of the pit. In addition a number of the fuses which would have been fitted to the bombs themselves were found, as well as the travelling plugs which fitted into the fuse mount on the bomb before it was fused. These plugs would have been discarded each time a bomb was fused and so offered direct evidence, along with the .303 ballistite (blank) rounds, of bombs being fired. Thus, apart from the tube of the mortar itself, we had found virtually all the components of the weapon and its ammunition. A re-examination of the corrugated iron from the roof also showed clear evidence of explosive damage on its front edge, indicating that there had been an explosion in the pit. Had it been hit by retaliatory artillery fire or had there been a catastrophic accident with a toffee-apple? We will never know. What we do know is that the Ulster Division attack on 1 July 1916 was supported by a 'hurricane' mortar bombardment. The manufacturing date found on the

This encrusted lump is made up of Stokes mortar safety pins, probably used in the bombardment of Vimy Ridge in April 1917. Note how the rings are looped together in pairs. The two rusted objects to the left are fuse assemblies from the bombs themselves. (*DRK*)

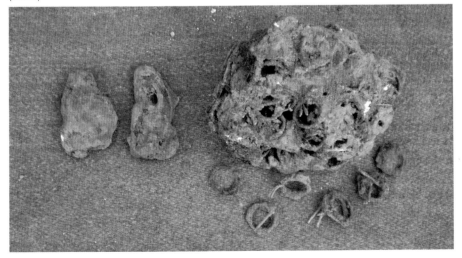

bombs was February 1916, so it is quite possible that we had uncovered a weapon and its pit used in support of that attack.

A similar story was pieced together from the results of the dig at Vimy Ridge, where a section of support-line trench was excavated. Large numbers of split-pins with a ring at one end started to come out of the fill of the trench. At first it was thought that these had come from Mills bombs, but as more and more were found it was noticed that they were often rusted together in pairs. The Mills bomb, of course, only has one split-pin, whereas the 3-inch and 4-inch Stokes mortar round has two. One retains a fly-off lever which arms the bomb as it leaves the mortar tube, and the second secures the detonation system itself. A search was made straight away through the documentary material concerning the site gathered before the excavation started (and stored in a box in the back of the project Land Rover). Sure enough, a hurricane bombardment by Stokes mortars had taken place from precisely this location on the morning of 9 April 1917, in support of the Canadian attack on the mine craters opposite. The intensity of this bombardment became obvious shortly afterwards when a rusted lump, about half the size of a football, was found, which consisted entirely of Stokes' mortar pins. There must have been at least one hundred pins in the lump. Clearly many rounds had been fired in a short space of time from this location, and rather than discarding the pins on to the floor, the gunners had collected them into a sandbag, which had then been lost or thrown away. Further confirmation came a short distance along the trench where a cache of the mortar rounds themselves was found, protected by a partially collapsed timber and tar-paper shelter. These rounds were unfired, with their safety rings still in place. In this particular case, because the Canadian advance was so rapid on that day, and the ground was not fought over again during the war, we can be fairly confident that these excavated items do indeed relate directly to the events described in the history books and to the hurricane bombardment of 9 April in particular. This was a rare but satisfying example of the direct conjunction of history and archaeology.

Perhaps two of the most iconic new technologies of the Great War were gas and tanks. The first use of chlorine gas by the German army at Ypres in May 1915 caught the Allied armies totally unprepared. However, the response was rapid and an array of respirators or gas masks was issued within days of the threat becoming clear. Early respirators were made from fabric, with cotton waste pads soaked in a variety of liquids designed to filter out or form a barrier to the deadly gas (in an emergency it was even suggested that a urine-soaked sock might

Team member and researcher Alastair Fraser experiments with a reproduction of the 'PH Hood' – the early pattern of gas-mask in use during the opening stages of the Somme battle. (*DRK*)

offer some protection if held over the nose and mouth, although you would have to be pretty desperate to resort to this expedient).

Even in wet conditions it seemed unlikely that such items would survive in a condition to be identified archaeologically. However, elements of even very early masks have been uncovered in excavation. The 'Hypo' helmet of mid-1915 consisted principally of a cloth bag fitted either with a broad single rectangular celluloid eyepiece or with two smaller ones with a gap for the nose; these were stitched into the bag that formed the respirator. The intention was that this would be worn over the head and tucked into the neck of the wearer's tunic. He could then both breathe and see sufficiently well to be still able to use his weapon. The idea was that air would be drawn in and expelled through the weave of the bag itself, which was treated with special chemicals. A surprising number of these 'plastic' eye-piece sheets have been recovered, and even if the bag has long since rotted away there is always a distinctive double line of machine stitching and the faint impression of the fabric pattern present on the celluloid. These items are small, fragile and easily overlooked, and if allowed to dry out become very brittle, but careful digging has brought them to light.

One might wonder why such a valuable and life-saving piece of equipment might be abandoned, but the answer is simply progress. By September 1915 British troops had received the improved PH helmet

Excavated fragments of a PH Hood from Thiepval Wood. The eyepieces and breathing valve survive although the flannel hood itself has rotted. These have proved to be common finds on all the team's excavations. (The unrelated object on the right is a tin of boot dubbin, still with usable dubbin in it.) (*DRK*)

that included a no-return or flutter valve that was placed in the mouth. This meant that the wearer breathed in through an improved double-layer fabric hood, but was able to expel carbon dioxide by blowing through the non-return valve (held in the teeth) without any danger of accidentally breathing in gas. This respirator also featured two glass eyepieces with a surrounding screw thread that sandwiched the layers of fabric. Once again it is the metal, glass and rubber elements that are found archaeologically. Examples of these have been discovered on almost every excavation carried out by the team, for example at Forward Cottage near Ypres and at Thiepval.

Not all gas used in the war was lethal. The Germans in particular made wide use of non-lethal irritant agents such as tear gas, which affected the eyes. It is an often forgotten point that saturating an area you wished to capture with lethal agents, or with long-lived agents such as mustard gas, would be counter-productive as your own troops would then have to occupy the gas-filled trenches after the enemy had been driven out. This explains why the British soldier from the Kings Own Lancaster Regiment whose remains were excavated at Serre (described in more detail in a later chapter) had with him both a PH hood and gas goggles when he was discovered in October 2003. The latter were intended as a protection against these non-lethal agents. Had this soldier

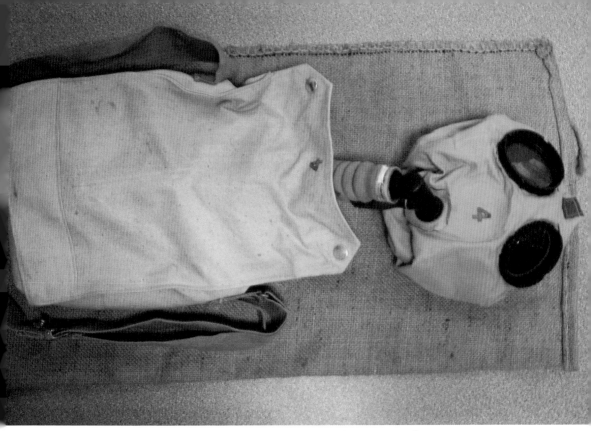

This replica example of the British Small Box Respirator demonstrates the sophistication of anti-gas measures achieved by the autumn of 1916. Little survives of the fragile 'gas masks' after nearly ninety years underground. (*ASR/RLC Museum*)

served for only a few more months, he would have received the final anti-gas product of the British army during the war, the Small Box Respirator (or SBR) which entered general service from September 1916.

This is the familiar gas mask with round eye-pieces and a corrugated tube connecting it to a separate filter. No parts of SBR kits have yet been found in excavation, but this may simply reflect the fact that most of the team's sites so far have focused on the early part of the war (although this kit was available in time for the Vimy battle in April 1917). Maybe one will be uncovered in the future.

Finally of course we come to the tank. The team has not yet had the chance to look for one of these monsters, but perhaps surprisingly they do survive buried on the battlefield. This was demonstrated a few years ago at Cambrai by Philippe Gorczynski, who, after years of painstaking research into the movements and fates of the 300 or so tanks involved in that battle, was able to identify the resting-place of one almost complete tank. After a significant amount of effort and expense he was able to recover this vehicle, and it is hoped that it will go on public display in due course. However, smaller but equally compelling evidence of tank fighting can be found on that battlefield if you know where to look. The majority of the tanks which broke down or were destroyed during the battle were salvaged by one side or the other. The Germans captured a number of tanks as a consequence of their counter-attack in early December, and several of these were taken away for analysis. In order to prevent some of the broken-down tanks from falling into German hands, they were deliberately blown up by the retreating British. Using his encyclopaedic knowledge of the battle Philippe was able to take the authors to the temporary resting-place of one such tank. He described how on the day of the battle a tank from G Battalion had reached that point before being knocked out, and subsequently was destroyed by the Royal Engineers. Superficially there was nothing to see, we were simply standing at the corner of an ordinary-looking farmer's field. However, as soon as we walked around a bit it became obvious that the ploughsoil was full of small metal fragments. We showed Philippe a short length of brass tubing about the size of your little finger. He identified it as part of the radiator of the tank in question. It was a remarkable find after ninety years on the surface.

This experience shows that in addition to the remains left in the formal trench systems that were occupied for periods of weeks or months, evidence sometimes survives of events which took place outside the trenches and lasted only for a few hours or minutes. Virtually everything that happened in the war has left a physical trace, albeit the trace may sometimes be very slight. All you need is a trained eye, and sufficient documentary background research, to find it. Of course, if you can find a local man who has made it the subject of his life's work, this process can be greatly speeded up!

Chapter 5

Death in the Trenches

THE COST

Death or injury in war is random, and although few soldiers believe that they will die many fear being wounded, especially in a way that might leave them disabled. In every war ever fought the first casualties have been caused accidentally, either in training or on the approach to battle. Many soldiers died in their home countries when grenades exploded prematurely on the bombing range, and nervous sentries shot hundreds when they failed to hear their frightened response to a challenge in the dead of night. It is a grim fact that half the casualties suffered by the Royal Flying Corps were the result of flying accidents when the pilots were in training. To these losses can be added the men who died from the diseases and illnesses common in the civilian population, or suffered from disorders that would have proved fatal whether they had served in the army or not. Simple bad planning caused a few tragic cases. In 1915 British volunteers died from cold when they paraded in a snowstorm on Epsom Downs for an inspection by Lord Kitchener. His late arrival condemned many willing volunteers to death from hypothermia even before they saw a German soldier.

Figures derived from the British Medical Service volume *Medical Services, Casualties and Medical Statistics* tell their own grim story.[15] Between 1914 and 1918 the British army on the Western Front suffered 3,528,486 non-battle casualties (including death, injury and periods 'on the sick' through accident and disease) compared to 2,690,054 inflicted in battle. In these figures the term casualty refers not only to the dead but also to the wounded and sick. Clearly more combat casualties would be likely to be fatal, but simply being in the army, crowded together in insanitary conditions and surrounded by lethal weapons, was a dangerous business even before the enemy was taken into consideration. This is not to suggest that the BEF was profligate with the lives of its men (as it has suited some historians to argue); on the contrary, standards were actually very high. The Great War is notable as the first major conflict where combat fatalities in the military exceeded those due to disease (excepting military and civilian losses in the 'flu pandemic of 1918). Only thirteen years earlier in South Africa British and Dominion forces had lost 7,000 men dead in combat, and another 14,000 from disease, a ratio of two to one. Standards of hygiene and medical care had come a long way in a decade.

Once soldiers came close to the enemy the probability of injury or death increased to a greater or lesser degree depending upon the type of sector in which the men were serving and whether an attack was planned. It is a curious point that the Somme sector in 1915 was regarded as cushy, compared to the region around Ypres. In the following year this situation had changed considerably. But even if the sector were quiet and the enemy troops not too aggressive, casualties would still occur as snipers, random shelling and raids took their toll. Even if you did not volunteer for a patrol you might be selected for a wiring party in no-man's-land, where a few hours spent trying to silently erect barbed wire entanglements while continually under the threat of enemy flares exposing you and your comrades to rifle, machine-gun and artillery fire was sufficient to prove that death could strike at any moment.

In the trenches smoke from a cooking fire or showing a shovel over the parapet could provoke trench mortar fire or artillery which might find victims even if the soldiers took shelter in a dug-out. The result of this attrition was that even in a cushy sector a certain number of men would be killed or wounded every day. It has been calculated that during the period of routine trench warfare from mid-December 1915 up until the first day of the battle of the Somme, casualties in the BEF were in excess of 125,000 men. This can be broken down to a little less than 4,500 casualties per week, at a time when no major offensive action was happening. Once battle began these figures were dwarfed, and during the first three days of the battle 13 per cent of the British soldiers involved in the battle became casualties.[16] This, however, is a lower figure than the 14.30 per cent inflicted on the British army in late July and early August 1917 during the third battle of Ypres, but it is dwarfed by the staggering 36 per cent suffered by the British 5th Army in late March and early April 1918 at the time of the German offensive.

These figures can be broken down further. Only 7.61 per cent of the wounded and less than 1 per cent of the sick died after reaching medical units. In consequence, 82 per cent of the wounded returned to some form of duty, as did 93 per cent of the sick. Thus eight out of ten who made it to a doctor would live. During the entire war the British Empire as a whole suffered 975,399 deaths from a mobilised force of 8,837,000 men and women. Hence around 10.7 per cent of those who served in the armed forces died. It also means that despite the total casualties of 3,280,408, more than eight out of ten servicemen and women went home. The vast cemeteries that dot the battlefield of the Great War represent a significant minority of those who served there, but not the majority that popular opinion might suggest. France, however, suffered 1,397,800 dead, more than 16 per cent of those who served, and Germany, with an army that was broadly on the strategic defensive for most of the war, 13.6 per cent.

THE WOUNDED

For reasons that are both humanitarian and psychological, the presence of wounded men on the battlefield or in a defended position weakens the resolve of others to fight. In some circumstances this can demoralise a unit when the men realise that medical care is not available. Soldiers need the reassurance that such care is available should the worst happen if they are going to maintain their resolve to stay in action. For these reasons, together with the high probability of the return to action of those wounded who were rapidly provided with medical attention, the system of treatment in all armies was based on rapid evacuation from the battle zone combined with appropriate medical care along this 'chain' of movement.

The most advanced elements of this chain were the stretcher-bearers, drawn in the British and German forces from the parent unit but in the French army separate volunteers. All soldiers held these non-combatant stretcher-bearers in the highest regard, and in the French army the 'brancardiers' were often men who for whatever reason would not take human life, but would save it. Sadly many of these men had little medical training, and the shortage of transport in the French army early in the war and of basic medical supplies for the German army in 1917 and 1918 meant that evacuation of the wounded could be excruciatingly painful. The protection for stretcher-bearers was no more than an armband carrying the red Geneva Cross or the 'SB' of the British stretcher-bearers. In battle these men would follow the advancing units into no-man's-land or venture into the trenches while the fighting raged to treat the wounded with initial 'first aid', before recovering them by

An RAMC orderly (distinguished by his Geneva Cross armband) provides a drink at a wounded collecting post at Beaumont Hamel on 1 July 1916. A regimental stretcher-bearer (with an SB armband) sits nearby. (*Imperial War Museum: Q739*)

means of stretchers (or on their own backs) to a place of relative safety.

Every soldier was issued with a bandage of some sort that was either slipped into an outer pocket or in the case of the British sewn into the skirt of the tunic, so every man knew where this vital item was to be found. If it was possible to do so, a wounded soldier was initially supposed to treat his own wounds to staunch the flow of blood and stop the entry of bacteria into the wound. Very often a comrade would assist him, and this might be enough to allow the wounded man to make his way to the rear. These 'walking wounded' were a major component of the early arrivals at hospital during battle as they had the advantage of mobility. Those soldiers who were unable to walk had to wait for the stretcher-bearers, who often could not reach the wounded until after nightfall. Equipped with a stretcher, blankets, a water-proof sheet and large 'shell dressings' to treat wounds that were too big for the 'first field dressing', the stretcher-bearers would do what they could to prevent further blood loss, splint broken limbs and deal with shock. Wounded soldiers are always thirsty and eager for reassurance, so large water-bottles were carried by those caring for the injured. It was a common practice at the time to provide the wounded with a cigarette to help 'calm their nerves' and this familiar act, health issues aside, often had a remarkably soothing effect on shocked and frightened soldiers.

Once his wounds had received this initial, if basic, treatment, the injured man, minus his weapons and equipment but retaining his helmet and respirator (gas mask), would be carried to the closest medical position. In most armies this consisted of little more than an aid post established by the regimental or battalion medical officer. This would be, usually, in a dug-out in the second-line trenches. Known as a *Trupenverbandplatz* (Aid Post) in the German army and as a Regimental Aid Post in the British forces, this was where the first doctor would be encountered. These exposed positions put the doctors in great danger – which was heightened by the risks some of them took in going forward to treat the wounded on the battlefield. As a result the British army lost over 900 doctors, and the only double recipients of the Victoria Cross were in the Royal Army Medical Corps.

Each forward doctor would have a very small team of medical assistants and a limited range of medical supplies, comforts and extra rations available. His

The standard field dressing was carried by every British soldier in a pocket inside his tunic. It was used by the soldier or his mates to stem bleeding and keep the wound fairly clean. The larger shell dressing was used by stretcher-bearers together with iodine contained in a glass phial to deal with larger wounds often caused by shell splinters. (*ASR/RLC Museum*)

The well-visited grave of Noel Chavasse RAMC in Brandhoek New Military Cemetery near Ypres in Belgium. His two VC awards (the second posthumous) are clearly inscribed on the headstone. (*DRK*)

job was to assess the patient and ensure that he was able to withstand the journey away from the battlefield to the next, larger, medical post. It was at this time that a wounded soldier would receive pain relief, might have his dressings checked and adjusted, and perhaps receive an injection of anti-tetanus serum. Here also an NCO from the medical service would usually enter all the patient's details on to a Field Medical Card that would travel with him. This helped to ensure that the doctors further to the rear were aware of the patient's injuries and what treatment he had already received. Patients were kept at this forward post for the briefest possible time before being evacuated by stretcher. Walking wounded were directed to make their own way to the rear to a collecting post established for those who did not require stretcher or ambulance transport.

Evidence of a medical officer at work was uncovered at Beaumont Hamel, where the excavations revealed not only an RAMC officer's tunic button, but also an ampoule containing sterile suture, part of a thermometer and a tin of iodine ampoules.

Every soldier carried a single iodine ampoule to place on his field dressing before applying it to his wound, but tins of them were only carried by medical officers, and thus such an officer had clearly been in the area. It was tempting to link these items to the events of 1 July 1916, and the relevant television episode of *Trench Detectives* did so, telling the story of Lieutenant Walmsley of the Border Regiment, a man of

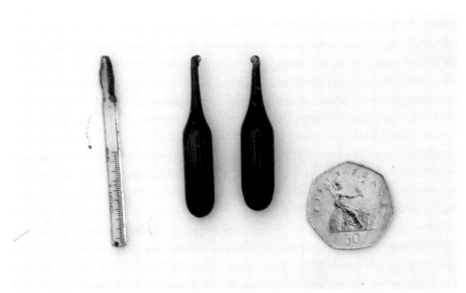

A fragment of a medical thermometer and several iodine ampoules, still with their contents intact, found at Beaumont Hamel. This is clear evidence that a regimental medical officer was at work in the area. (*DRK*)

strong religious conviction who had given up service as a Methodist missionary in China to serve at the front. We do not know that the items belonged to him, and indeed we never claimed this (despite what some of our critics have asserted), but rather, as is often the case in Great War archaeology, the objects served to illuminate a story told in the documentary history. Who knows, it might have been his button, since we know he was there on 1 July. The discovery of the medical items also led to the memorable television moment of one of the authors becoming hopelessly over-excited on camera.

For the wounded the next stage in the evacuation chain could be the most difficult, if not for the patients then for the stretcher-bearers who had to carry their heavy and inert loads along narrow trenches, sometimes deep in mud, often in pitch darkness and always at risk of enemy fire. Although bearer posts were established at which exhausted men could rest while others took over the patient, the endurance of these men is one of the most under-estimated aspects of the war. The cellar at Avril Williams' guest-house in Auchonvillers bears the graffiti of several stretcher-bearers who scratched their names and army numbers into the chalk of the wall, possibly while waiting for duty in the communication trench outside. Many men owed their lives to the dedication of the medical services that brought them back to the relative safety of the

Advanced Dressing Station or Collecting Post whatever the conditions. It was here, in a dug-out or shell-proof cellar a kilometre or so behind the line, that a larger team of doctors, bearers and dressers, from the Field Ambulance in British service and the *Sanitatskompagnie* ('Bearer Company') in German, was available to provide treatment. As at the Regimental Aid Post, surgery was not usually available and the emphasis was on ensuring that the patient was warm, dry, free from pain and not losing blood. By 1916 this is also where fractured limbs would be stabilised.

From the ADS or CP a severely injured patient might be taken directly to a Main Dressing Station if surgery was immediately required, but in most cases the wounded were sent by motor ambulance, light train or tramway to a Casualty Clearing Station or *Feldlazarette* ('Field Hospital'). This was remote from the battlefield, reasonably safe and housed in a tented or hutted camp usually close to a railway or canal system. With between 200 and 300 beds in both the German and the British services, this was where specialist treatment was received. Some CCSs specialised in surgical procedures, with head, chest, limb and other wounds being dealt with by specific units staffed by a surgical specialist, assisted by nurses, laboratories and the latest equipment of rapidly improving patterns. It was here that patients usually received blood transfusions and were X-rayed prior to treatment. Among the great medical advances of the conflict were the use of blood transfusion, plastic surgery and the common use of X-rays. Some CCSs specialised in 'shell shock', and the 'talking therapy' meant that over 80 per cent of these physiological cases returned to active duty.

It would often be at a CCS that most British wounded met a chaplain, but in forces with a large Catholic element the chaplains would be up with the forward troops to provide spiritual support to the dying and absolution to the dead. It is to the credit of the Roman Catholic Church that its priests with the BEF had free rein to go wherever they felt most needed on the battlefield, while the Church of England restricted its clerics to rear areas. Thus many a man who would have been wary of any church, let alone that of Rome, received vital help and comfort (not to mention free cigarettes) from the brave and selfless Catholic padres well forward in the trenches.

The evacuation chain, of course, required the 'sorting' of casualties. The system called 'triage' by the French categorised the wounded and indicated both where they should be treated and whether it was worthwhile.

This system produced the so-called 'moribund' ward in which patients who were expected to die rapidly, or who could not be treated without using large quantities of resources better employed on patients who might recover and return to the battlefield, were provided with comfort and pain relief, but little else. It is worth noting that a severely injured patient received on a quiet day at a CCS when there were few casualties could expect to receive the best treatment available. However, the same patient arriving during a major battle might find himself regarded as moribund. This had serious ethical implications and doctors of the time expended a great deal of time on debating this deviation from civilian medical ethics. Added to this, speed of evacuation could be an issue. During a large battle, even if the evacuation chain did not break down, the numbers of wounded being received could clog the system. On 1 July 1916 one Assistant Director of Medical Services near the town of Albert, who was normally a medical administrator, was reduced to giving the wounded drinks from a tin mug and bucket as they lay in the town square waiting for ambulances. By contrast the following year the casualties from the early phases of the battle of Arras in April 1917 were arriving in London by special ambulance trains shortly after lunchtime on the day that they were wounded.

CCSs were not true hospitals but they prepared casualties for onward movement to a Base Hospital or *Kriegslazarette* ('War Hospital') in German service. These stationary hospitals dealt with long-term care and rehabilitation of the wounded. Some in British service were in France and Belgium, while others were back in the United Kingdom. Many stately homes and hotels became temporary hospitals dealing with thousands of casualties during the course of the war.

Some of these hospitals became specialist units, with Queen Mary's Hospital at Sidcup dealing with plastic and reconstructive surgery, and Roehampton becoming a centre for the fitting of artificial limbs. One of the features of the wartime scene in all of the combatant nations was the presence of recovering wounded soldiers in parks, pubs and theatres. In British service these men wore a distinctive blue uniform with white shirt and red tie. As might be imagined, these men evoked sympathy and compassion from civilians, but all knew that once they had recovered they would return to the front or to a labour unit if medically downgraded. Only a small percentage were invalided out, but with armies consisting of millions of men this meant hundreds of thousands of disabled.

Private John Andrew Robertshaw in hospital blues after being wounded in September 1917. He was back at the front in early 1918 serving with the 10th Battalion East Yorkshire Regiment ('Hull Commercials'). (*ASR*)

THE DEAD

Unlike the wounded soldier, who had to be removed from the battlefield as quickly as possible, the dead could be dealt with over a period of time. The degree of care taken varied according to the military situation and might result in nothing being done at all. On other occasions bodies had to be dealt with rapidly, for example if they were physically in the way in a confined post or looked especially distressing, or in periods of hot weather when decomposition would take place very quickly.

The dead fell roughly into three categories: those that died or were killed in a position held by friendly troops; those that were killed in no-man's-land (or outside the trench system but on the battlefield); and those who died behind the lines. The last group included all those soldiers who were killed by long-range shelling or bombing in areas outside direct enemy observation, or succumbed to their wounds while in the chain of evacuation provided for the wounded. The last group can perhaps be judged to be the most fortunate of the dead, because the soldiers dealing with them had the opportunity to establish their identity from their papers or identity discs and to bury them in properly marked graves, usually in an appropriate military cemetery. Often these burials were accompanied by a religious ceremony of some sort, although this may only have been a few words spoken over each body by a busy military chaplain. Men who died in more dangerous or inaccessible places naturally received less attention.

One of the features of the battlefields today is the presence of cemeteries with names that include ADS (Advanced Dressing Station) or CCS (Casualty Clearing Station). These were the cemeteries established immediately outside the medical units and reflect the large number of men who did not survive the journey towards the base hospitals and 'Blighty'. Shock, blood loss and infection all killed men on occasions, even when the wound itself was apparently not severe. Examples of this kind of cemetery include Essex Farm ADS near Ypres, Auchonvillers Military Cemetery on the Somme close to an underground Collection Post, and those at Brandhoek on the road between Poperinge and Ypres which were based on specialist CCSs.

The vast Tyne Cot cemetery, the product of the third battle of Ypres, was based around a Regimental Aid Post situated in a captured German pillbox. The haphazard layout of the burials next to the Cross of Sacrifice at the core of the cemetery is the result of night-time burials in improvised graves, while the post-war interments lie in organised rows round about. This cemetery also includes German soldiers who were wounded and made prisoner by the British, and who died while receiving medical attention. This largely explains the presence of other nationalities in cemeteries, but this may also sometimes be the result of 'concentration'. When the war ended many burials were scattered over a wide area of the battlefields and others remained missing. In a logical manner the decision was taken by the then Imperial War Graves Commission that these dispersed burials and temporary cemeteries, that were sometimes in the middle of villages, should be brought together into larger cemeteries. These would be both easier to maintain and more convenient for families to visit. This explains the size of Tyne Cot, to which bodies were brought from all over that part of the Ypres Salient. The same process was applied by other Allied nations involved in the war. However, while France and Belgium were happy to grant space for the graves of the Allied dead, they were less willing to give any more land than was totally necessary to the German dead. As a result this process of concentration was rigorously applied to the German dead, which explains the apparently crammed nature of many of the cemeteries maintained by the *Volksbund Deutsche Kriegsgräberfürsorge* (VDK), the German equivalent of the CWGC.

While this concentration process was being carried out, the battlefields were also searched for the missing; if located, British dead would be given a burial with their comrades. In contrast the French, following Catholic practice, erected a vast ossuary at Verdun in which the remains of their dead were interred in a way similar to the catacombs. Thousands of sets of partial and complete human remains are entombed in a concrete structure equipped with viewing windows for visitors. This process of searching the battlefield was not carried out in a single survey. In the period between the end of the Great War and the beginning of the Second World War in 1939, teams from the Army and IWGC combed the battlefields no fewer than three times. The Imperial War Museum holds maps from this period in which the number of bodies to be found in each area of ground are categorised. By the spring of 1921 the War Graves Commission had established over a thousand cemeteries that were judged fit to be visited.

In battle it was simple logic that those men who died in a friendly trench or position would be dealt with first, but probably not until night fell. Unlike a wounded comrade, who would have received immediate attention and for whom another soldier may have risked his own life, a dead man had no claim on a soldier's attention. As a result bodies might be pushed up out of the trench on to the parapet or parados, in front or

German medical orderlies outside a ruined church somewhere on the Western Front. Unlike the British, all German soldiers involved in medical care wore the Geneva cross armband, and as can be seen here occasionally carried weapons. (*ASR*)

behind the position, or simply covered with a blanket, *zeltbahn* or groundsheet. In some cases this luxury was not available and a handkerchief or sandbag was used to cover the head of the deceased so that a familiar face could be hidden from sight until nightfall. For reasons of sanitation, and in observation of religious practice, armies laid down rules on where bodies should be buried. The orders for Trench Routine produced by the 41st Division in late 1916 specified that 'Dead are to be buried at the place appointed by brigade headquarters'. However, the conditions of trench warfare, including the problem of moving even the recently dead on stretchers, meant that many soldiers killed in the trenches were buried close to where they fell, sometimes in a convenient shell hole or disused trench or in a hastily dug grave. It is typically these impromptu burials that have been uncovered by the team in excavation. Remains have been found placed in shell holes, and in one case in a mass grave in a backfilled trench. This is discussed in more detail in the next chapter.

Bodies are always heavy and difficult to move, even by fit soldiers, and the process of decay can be rapid. As a result, although in theory a single soldier can carry or pull a comrade, morality and common sense meant that the body would usually be stripped of its equipment and weapons. These could be taken over by his comrades or reissued after being processed by the units established to salvage such items. To assist in the process of moving the body, a man's groundsheet was very convenient, being both durable and waterproof and providing some of the functions of a shroud. The process of decomposition could be hastened by the addition of chloride of lime to the bodies before they were covered with earth, and stocks of this corrosive powder were kept close to the front line and brought up into the trenches when required. Sadly, all too frequently such burials were shallow, and the smell of decomposition attracted flies and rats, which would burrow down to a hasty burial. If this was not bad enough, subsequent shelling could also bring remains to the surface, an experience described by Wilfred Owen in 1917 when a fellow officer of the Manchester Regiment, whom Owen knew well, was disinterred by a shell and lay 'in various places round about'.[17]

Rats, maggots and further damage to the human body were not only the preserve of soldiers buried close to the defended positions. The fate of soldiers killed in no-man's-land, either in an attack, on patrol or during a raid, was the most uncertain. When the British took over the sector of the front near Vimy in 1916 one feature was nicknamed 'Zouave Valley', because it was still littered with the remains of these

North African soldiers killed more than a year earlier. Their bodies were already reduced to skeletons, but their distinctive red trousers were a tragic and colourful feature of the landscape. In some cases individuals were quite distinctive and became almost familiar to the soldiers. Men going on patrol in a featureless piece of no-man's-land were sometimes told to turn at 'the body of the German with a beard' or to go no further than the French officer. It is perhaps not surprising that these instructions were given by British soldiers, as in their hierarchy of attention it was the British dead who merited burial first.

Before the dead soldier was buttoned or tied into a covering sheet or blanket, an attempt would be made to establish his identity. This would involve searching through his pockets for a pay book or papers. This process was not popular with those given the task, and the search was usually restricted to looking for the man's identity tag, which was usually worn on a cord around the neck and rested between the tunic and shirt on the upper chest. German and French identification tags were metal, hence the term 'Dog Tag' which was introduced by German troops in Prussia who had to wear this item, as they felt like dogs. British tags were metal discs at the start of the war, but became vulcanised fibre as the army expanded. This choice of cheaper material had obvious implications for durability as vulcanised fibre can both rot and burn. As an aside, a feature of the limited number of casualties excavated by the team is the quantity of personal items associated with each set of remains. It has long been argued that bodies were routinely looted by other soldiers, but at least for our casualties this appears not to have been the case as watches and money were found on several occasions, although whether this was due to altruism or to the state of decomposition of the remains is not clear.

A second problem was the wearing of a single tag. If this was removed from the body either at the point of burial or when the body was discovered, it became virtually impossible to establish the identity of the soldier when he was either disinterred or found by a burial party. This problem became clear after the failed British attack on the Somme left bodies in no-man's-land. Although the identity tags were soon recovered, the remains were left where they fell. Many would not be buried until the spring of 1917, when they were marked as an unknown soldier of their particular regiment, as it was possible to determine their unit from buttons and badges, but not to discover an individual's name. As a result the British began issuing a second, octagonal, tag, which was meant to be removed from a dead soldier, leaving the other round one for subsequent identification. The German army went over to using a similar system, in which the tag had duplicate information separated by perforations in the metal. This meant that the lower half could be broken off, leaving the upper section in position around the wearer's neck.

Despite this improvement, soldiers were realistic about the possibility of their body being dismembered and many soldiers purchased non-regulation tags made from coins or scrap material and wore them around the wrist as an insurance against their future death. This pragmatic act, which was carried out by soldiers of all ranks and of all nationalities, indicates to us the importance men placed upon their future identification and the fear they shared of burial in an unnamed grave. Similarly, soldiers also went to great lengths to erect a cross or

A probably posed photograph of a German soldier in position next to an unburied corpse, perhaps that of a French soldier, based on the Adrian helmet lying nearby. Such images have become iconic and form a key part of the public perception of the conflict. (*Taylor Library*)

marking on even the most hasty burial, to ensure that the place could be identified in future. There were no obvious markers close to the excavated remains of the two German soldiers buried at Serre, but such markers might well have been made of wood, and were either destroyed in the fighting or scavenged for fuel during the winters that followed by soldiers more concerned about a hot meal than the fate of a soldier who was beyond help. A single support for barbed wire, a 'silent picket', was found alongside the British soldier discovered there and it is possible to speculate that at some point this marked his crude burial, the most military of temporary memorials. Sadly the intensity of the fighting meant that not only did many individual burial markers disappear, but so too did entire cemeteries. This explains the notice in some cemeteries stating that certain soldiers are 'known to be buried here'; the army may well have retained a list of who was buried in the cemetery, but with the markers gone it was impossible to tell which grave was which.

Whether a soldier was given a formal burial or not, once his death had been established by means of his papers, identification tags or post-battle interview with his comrades, his family had to be informed. This would be linked to the military process by which the dead soldier would cease to be paid. However, a pension or compensation would be due to the closest relatives. The usual way in which this news arrived would be a letter, or in the case of officers a telegram from the military authorities stating that the soldier had been killed or had died on such a date. Very often these messages were very short on detail and it would take some time before any other information arrived. This usually took the form of a letter from a soldier's superior officer in which phrases such as 'he died instantly' or 'his last words were of you' were used regardless of the reality of the situation. Sometimes, however, surprising amounts of detail were provided. In one case one of the authors was shown a letter written to the parents of a deceased gunner by the commanding officer of one of the two 14-inch railway guns. In it he explained that the young man had been killed when the mechanical breech closed and crushed him to death, but he commented that the gun had remained in action thereafter.

In other cases a soldier's comrades might take it upon themselves to write to a widow or grieving parents. Occasionally a loyal comrade would give up some of his own home leave to visit the bereaved family. These visits were not always welcome, and served only as a reminder of the loss and the circumstances that had deprived the family of a member, while leaving his comrade unharmed. It was not unusual for such visitors to bring home personal items, as the army was anxious to restore personal effects to the family. Most frequently this was done by post and tragic parcels of privately owned items, especially those of officers who had equipped themselves at their own expense, were received by hundreds of thousands of families. It might appear surprising to us that items covered in blood or pierced by bullets had to be returned, but as recently as 1982 the cap of one of the officers of the *Atlantic Conveyor*, which was sunk in the Falklands conflict, was sent to his family still wet with water from the ocean in which he had drowned.

Despite such letters or visits, many families wanted more detail and wrote to the War Office or Red Cross for more information, both to reassure themselves about the circumstances of the death and to confirm that it had indeed been their son, husband or father that had died. Despite this, many people believed, especially when there was no grave to visit, that the soldier would come home at some point. Hospital treatment records were maintained, and the Red Cross also kept a record of the detailed fates of soldiers, but most of this data was destroyed at the end of the war, and what survived was kept confidential as it was thought too distressing to be openly available. The records of the Australian Red Cross survive, although these too were kept under lock and key for fear of causing distress to relatives, although now the information is being made accessible to next of kin. Sadly the anodyne letters saying that loved ones had 'died instantly' and 'didn't suffer' often hid a much more painful truth.

THE 'MISSING'

Clearly, given the situation described earlier in this chapter, the battlefields of the Great War still conceal the buried remains of many soldiers. Any visitor is also forcefully confronted with the idea of the 'Missing' by the great memorials such as Thiepval, which records the names of 73,000 men who 'were denied the known and honoured burial given to their comrades', or the Menin Gate in Ypres where another 55,000 names are recorded. It is one of the enduring popular ideas of the war that the conditions were so grim, both in terms of bottomless mud and endless artillery bombardment, that all these men simply disappeared. They were absorbed into this morass, somehow 'consumed' by a conflict that had taken on the character of a hungry monster. Much war literature and poetry develops this metaphor of the war needing somehow to be 'fed' with the lives of soldiers.

Inevitably, the truth of the matter is somewhat more complicated. The idea that men could simply disappear, and more importantly that the armies of the day would make no effort to find them or record their passing, is erroneous. Armies of all nations, however good or bad they were at fighting, were very good at counting. Returns and lists were created for everything from spoons to tanks, and men in particular were

The form of words used on the Menin Gate to describe those more commonly referred to as 'The Missing'. The emphasis on a 'known' place of burial is significant. Similar wording is used on the Thiepval Memorial. (*DRK*)

counted often, as they needed to be fed, paid, equipped, sent on leave or kept in the right place to fight. The recording of the dead was a critical part of this accounting process, if for no other reason than that the government resented paying wages to men who were no longer useful soldiers. Contrary to popular myth therefore, the armies paid very close attention to who was alive and who was dead.

Most armies in the Great War used a similar casualty recording system, which had been developed many years earlier. Casualties were generally divided into three categories:

Dead: this included those killed in action (KIA), those who died of their wounds (DOW) and those who died of disease (DOD).

Wounded: this included those evacuated to hospital as well as those treated within the unit, and again had various sub-categories.

Missing: those whose whereabouts after a battle were unknown.

It is the first and last categories that require further examination. In the world of 'Remembrance' the *Dead* are those in graves and the *Missing* are those with no known grave. This is not equivalent to the army system. The army system did not reflect anything to do with the final resting-place of a soldier's remains. A soldier was *Dead* either if his body was available to be examined, or if a colleague had seen him die and could vouch for his passing. A *Missing* soldier was one who might very well be dead but no one had witnessed it, or he might equally be a prisoner of war, a deserter, or simply lost and on his way back to the unit some days later. Much misunderstanding has developed from the confusion of this terminology.

A famous example of this was Private James McFadzean, who was present in Thiepval Wood with the 14th Royal Irish Rifles on 1 July 1916. On the way up to the attack several live grenades were dropped, and McFadzean immediately threw himself over the grenades to protect his comrades. He was subsequently awarded a posthumous Victoria Cross. At the time his body was placed on the parapet of the trench (he was not in the front line) to await later burial. His remains are now 'missing', but it is unlikely that means they remain to be found in the wood. Since his ID tag would have been removed immediately at the time of his death, possibly along with any significant personal effects, it is highly likely that a burial party did recover his remains but could not determine who he was. He could well therefore be in a nearby unnamed grave. At no time would the army have listed him as *Missing* since his death was clearly witnessed by a number of men.

Formally the men listed on the memorials to the 'Missing' are those with no known grave. This does not mean that their deaths were not observed and recorded, or indeed that they were not buried under a named marker by their comrades. It means only that when the cemeteries were consolidated after the war, and the lists drawn up, a grave with their name on it could not be identified. All Commonwealth cemeteries also contain gravestones bearing the words 'Known unto God' – in other words, soldiers whose name is unknown. Sometimes a rank and unit is recorded, but in other cases it was not possible even to determine the dead man's nationality. It is easy for visitors to the Thiepval memorial to assume that the 73,000 men whose names are recorded there were all lost into the morass of the Somme battlefield, and still lie under the ploughsoil awaiting discovery. This is not the case: many lie in 'Known unto God' graves in the surrounding cemeteries.

Thus when an attempt is made to quantify the soldiers whose remains are genuinely 'missing' in the landscape without a formal headstone or marker the mathematics becomes complex. The authors raised this

The headstone in Mill Road Cemetery, Thiepval, of Pte W. Stokes (Christian name unknown) of the West Riding Regiment. His family used the private text space to commemorate his older brother no. 240230 Pte John Henry ('Jack') Stokes of the same regiment who died the same day, but is 'Missing' and commemorated on the Thiepval Memorial. It is quite possible he lies under a 'Known unto God' headstone in the same cemetery. (*DRK*)

question with an official from the CWGC and received the answer that the calculation had never been done. This is fair enough as the CWGC is in the business of looking after the memorials, not searching for the dead, but it presents the archaeologist with a large unsolved question. Also, this discussion has so far only dealt with the remains of the victors. As was described in an earlier chapter, the situation for the Germans was a good deal worse. This was not because they had any lower standards of organisation or respect for the dignity of their own dead, but because once ejected from France and Belgium at the end of the war they had very little control over the permanent memorialisation of their grave sites.

THE ETHICS OF EXCAVATION

Any archaeologist digging on the Western Front has to acknowledge the fact that an unknown but significant number of soldiers' remains are likely to be present on any excavation site. In itself this is not a problem. Archaeologists are quite accustomed to dealing with human remains in the course of their work. Indeed, the search for the tombs of the ancients was one of the driving forces behind the development of the profession as a whole, and it is the 'grave-diggers' such as Howard Carter that occupy the largest place in the popular conception of archaeology. A significant portion of our understanding of past cultures is based on the excavation of the dead, to the extent that some ancient cultures are understood almost entirely through their funeral rites. For example, almost all surviving fragments of the language of the Etruscan civilisation of northern Italy come from grave markers and tombs. (Incidentally this has presented a significant obstacle to translation of the language, since the inscriptions, all of which contain variations on 'Here Lies Lucius . . .' do not give scholars much to work on.) Bodies themselves, therefore, are not a problem. Indeed, the public at large actually demands bodies from their archaeologists. The success of television programmes such as *Meet the Ancestors* or indeed *Finding the Fallen* testifies to this interest. The most famous archaeological discoveries over the last century were almost all of human remains: 'Oetzi', the frozen Bronze Age man from the Alps; 'Pete Marsh', the bog-body from Cheshire; or the poisoned sailors of the Franklin expedition. That the media sought to provide names for all these individuals, albeit fictional ones, is also significant. Nothing personalises the past in the public mind, paradoxically 'bringing it to life', more than a corpse, especially one with a name.

To what extent archaeology should be guided, or driven, by this popular fascination is, however, a moot point. The dead of all ages are entitled to at least the dignity and respect we would grant to our own departed, or indeed to be treated as we would like to be treated ourselves when we are gone. In practical terms the excavation of human remains is also a complex and expensive process if carried out with full archaeological rigour. As a result the archaeological community has developed an informal code of ethics over the years covering the remains of the dead. In the UK this is also constrained by the various legal requirements covering exhumation. Some of these laws date from the 1850s when their original intention was to prevent 'Burke and Hare'-style grave-robbing for the surgical trade, but many remain in force, and rightly so. The simplest and most widely encountered legislation actually makes it illegal for anyone, including an archaeologist, to exhume anyone, from any historical period, without a Home Office licence and permission from the coroner (although in practice these are issued to reputable archaeological groups by fax with a minimum of fuss).

The result of these ethical, legal and financial constraints is that contrary to popular belief archaeologists often seek to avoid digging up the dead, rather than the reverse; for them, the question is 'Why?' rather than 'Why not?' Two important reasons why human remains might be excavated are first, that their place of burial is under threat (they will be built over), and second, that they are from a period of history that means that their research value is sufficient to justify examining them. This means that non-Christian burials from early periods are often excavated as they are likely to contain objects which can tell us about the relevant culture, while Christians, who are typically buried with few grave-goods, are not. Under UK law Christians also receive preferential treatment, being legally entitled to be suitably reburied.

When it comes to the remains of the war dead these normal considerations are influenced by additional concerns, and some of the normal criteria for excavation are overturned. Some people believe that the presence of human remains on the battlefield makes it in some sense 'sacred' ground, and that the soldiers who lie there should be left to rest in peace without further disturbance. This opinion has been expressed to various members of the team, both personally and in letters and e-mails, and in some cases the point of view is passionately held (and at times angrily expressed). It is, however, only one point of view, and in our experience it is that of only a minority, and we ask those who hold that view to respect our right to differ from them. The concept that the battlefields can somehow be left untouched also comes up against the problem that was faced by the original proponents of the 'Zone Rouge' in 1919, that the land continues to be developed and cultivated, and thus the threat to the peace of the dead is on-going and increasing.

At the same time simply to search the battlefields for remains in order to generate archaeological 'stories' for public consumption would be equally unethical, and could be seen as pandering to the more prurient aspects of the public taste for archaeology. As a result the *No-Man's-Land* team has had to develop a code of ethics to deal with the remains of the dead from the Great War. This is a mixture of previously held moral conviction and an evolving response to experience on site, and while it suits us, and we would argue strongly for it, we don't expect everyone to agree with us.

Our foremost objective is to widen understanding of the Great War through excavation. Thus the criteria for site selection are based on what kind of archaeological remains we might find, including trenches, dug-outs or other interesting features. We do not go looking specifically for human remains. At the same time we acknowledge that they are likely to be uncovered. If a set of remains is found, the circumstances under which the remains came to be where they lie is of wider interest archaeologically, shedding light on how bodies were dealt with, or on how soldiers wore or chose personal equipment. However, this is not the main priority in excavating them. If a soldier is found, the over-riding priority is to ensure that his remains are as respectfully and completely as possible removed and passed on for proper reburial in a military cemetery. A key part of this process is the recovery of every scrap of evidence that might help to identify the soldier and allow him a named burial, and if possible the passing of this information to his family.

Once a set of remains has been disturbed, either on an archaeological site or accidentally, for example during construction work, the integrity of that burial has been broken. It is not possible to simply cover up or rebury a set of remains without possibly vital clues to the identity of that individual being lost. Also, as soon as they are exposed to the elements pieces of that evidence will start to degrade. Sadly also a set of exposed remains is a magnet for unscrupulous collectors and dealers who will strip a body of saleable items without regard to the fact that in so doing they may be stealing the only chance that soldier has of ever being identified. The result of this is that for the team any human remains uncovered on site immediately become the top priority, and all other work becomes secondary to their complete excavation and recording. Floodlights have been vital more than once, as it has become policy never to leave remains unattended, and where possible to complete their excavation in one session, no matter how long it takes. On several occasions the team has abandoned areas of planned excavation to avoid uncovering further bodies, and running the risk that time and money might run out with remains exposed but incompletely recovered.

Some might argue that digging people up when you find them, but not specifically looking for them while all the time digging in areas where they are likely to be found, is a somewhat nice distinction. However, it is impossible for archaeologists on the Western Front not to find remains, and in the authors' view a greater wrong would be committed by simply covering them up again. It is also hoped that by demonstrating that with close attention to detail and careful archaeology these men *can* often be identified, this will encourage those responsible for the many sets of remains found by chance in France and Belgium every year to take a bit more time and trouble over them. In short, we try to lead by example.

A powerful voice in this argument is that of the relatives of the soldiers concerned. As the next chapter will show, only in two cases so far has the team identified soldiers whose families were subsequently traced, but in both cases the response of the relatives was extremely positive. The families were both moved and excited by the discovery, if a little surprised, and it has led in one case to a re-establishment of links between the various branches of the family which had previously broken down. International friendships have also grown between the families and the excavation team members and researchers across the world. In our view there is no better tribute to the fallen than to establish links between the former belligerents and to increase our understanding of each other.

On a more personal level the team received a letter from an ex-serviceman who took great comfort from the idea that had he been so unfortunate as to fall in battle, there were those prepared to make this much effort to ensure that he received a proper burial. For the team this sentiment applies as much to those whose identities remain unknown as to those whose names were established. While the search for an identity is important, the claim of the individual to our care is undiminished even if he is reburied 'Known unto God'. The funeral described at the start of this book was one such, and while his case remains 'open' in terms of his identity, the satisfaction felt by the team members who attended his funeral was no less than it would have been had his name been on his headstone.

TECHNICALITIES

Having decided to excavate a set of remains, the next question is how to set about it and what types of information can be recovered. Some of the issues covered earlier in this book concerning context and artefacts are equally valid here, but in the case of human remains the information serves two purposes. First, an excavator is seeking to record how the remains arrived where they were found, along with a range of other general archaeological information, but secondly the question of identification is never far away. However, even soldiers whose identity is not established rapidly become individuals as aspects of their personal lives are revealed through pocket and pack contents, or peculiarities of equipment. The excavator is therefore quickly aware not just of the soldier in khaki or field grey, but also of the man within the uniform.

Much of the earlier ethical discussion concerns sets of human remains,

Hohenzollern Redoubt, Loos. Recording continues under floodlights late into the night of what proved to be the remains of only the lower half (hips and legs) of a British soldier. No identification was possible of these remains. (*LB*)

groups of bones which represent a single whole individual. In civilian archaeology it is normal to expect people to be buried in one piece, and if bits are missing it is usually because the remains have decayed very badly or have been disturbed later, for example by a wall foundation built through the grave. Sadly on Great War sites this is not the case. Frequently only parts of soldiers are found. At Loos the lower half of one British soldier was uncovered, from the hips down, recognisable by his British boots and parts of an issue small pack.

Nearby a single hand was found, with the finger bones lying in correct relationship to one another (what archaeologists refer to as 'articulated'), showing that when the hand was buried the bones were still held together by flesh and skin. Such fragments are a grisly reminder of the character of the war. At Vimy an area was excavated which appeared to be the remains of a sandbag wall. Within it were the remains of a British boot, containing the bones of part of a foot. In this case the toe had been cleanly sliced off the boot, and nothing was left above the ankle, suggesting that whoever filled that sandbag had inadvertently cut through the boot and shovelled it (either accidentally or deliberately) into the sandbag before it and its contents were used to build the wall.

Many of the accounts of life on the Western Front (such as that by Wilfred Owen referred to earlier) describe a situation where body parts lay around unburied, but to excavate them provides very immediate and quite shocking evidence of what these men described. Sometimes evidence of the almost complete destruction of a human being has been encountered. The only human remains uncovered at the Forward Cottage site near Ypres were a single molar tooth and a skull fragment the size of a large coin: not much to account for a human life. Where partial remains are found there is little the archaeologist can do, but as the proportion of the individual found increases so do the chances of identification. One of the real success stories of the team's work so far was the identification of Jakob Hönes, though even his remains were not complete. His body lay in a shallow shell hole mostly deep enough to survive undamaged, but his head, close to the surface, was missing, probably ploughed away during the eighty-eight years he had lain undiscovered. Ultimately the fact that the head was missing ceased to be relevant as enough was found to allow him to be identified, and thus to be returned to his family and buried.

The process of excavation of human remains is essentially quite simple, but requires a lot of time and patience. Basically the aim is to remove as much of the surrounding earth from whatever remains survive, usually bones, but to leave the bones sufficiently supported by the soil to stay in place in their various positions. The same applies to any objects which may be present. In the case of soldiers this means buttons, pieces of equipment and private items such as pocket or pack contents. Once this process is complete, the whole assemblage of objects and remains is photographed and recorded on scaled plans, as the location of the objects in relation to the body can be highly significant in telling their story.

Typically only one or two people can work on a single skeleton without the site becoming overcrowded, so the process cannot be rushed. Usually one complete skeleton will take a skilled excavator a day to uncover if it is relatively simply positioned, although more complex burials take longer. Mass graves in particular can become very complex as it is vital to establish from what may be a mass of intertwined limbs which bones belong to which individual and which objects are associated with each. This question was vital in the identification of the remains of Leopold Rothärmel (described fully in the following chapter). Here a number of men had been buried together, but several were not wearing their tunics, for reasons which still remain obscure. Instead these tunics had been thrown into the grave between and beside the bodies. Identification evidence was retrieved from the tunics, but to which body did they relate? In the end all of the sets of remains found in that part of the dig site were buried together in a single grave, with a marker indicating that Leopold and four other unknown soldiers were buried there. We don't know for sure which one he was, but we can be reasonably content he was one of them.

This painstaking process is made more difficult as time goes on because once a large part of the skeleton (or skeletons) is revealed it becomes increasingly difficult to reach the parts being worked on. Sometimes it is necessary to support the excavators on planks placed over the grave in order to reach the difficult places, and they might spend whole days lying on a plank working away carefully across a small area a few inches in front of their faces. Inevitably such work is a rather intimate experience for the archaeologist, probing between a stranger's ribs with a lollipop stick (wooden tools are often used as they do not damage fragile bone). Most archaeologists gain experience working on remains from the distant past and develop a certain detachment, but it is hard to maintain this on a Great War site. To be confronted at very close quarters not only with someone's personal things – the pipe in their pocket, or a postcard from home – but also with evidence of their violent death can be at times very difficult. Almost everyone in the team has had a moment during this process where they have had to stop and take a break, for fear that their emotions would overcome them. Sometimes also the state of preservation of the remains makes the process grim, since digging through hair and fingernails, or revealing evidence of maggot or rat infestation is never pleasant. However, the fact that we are affected by this work is key to understanding its importance. The day that uncovering the remains of soldiers leaves us unmoved emotionally is the day that we have lost something of our basic humanity, and it's time to find another job.

Work in the field is, however, only the first stage of the process. As soon as the plans have been drawn the artefacts and bones are bagged up and sent off to specialists. It has not always been possible to carry out a full pathological examination of the skeletons we have uncovered but in most cases at least a brief cleaning and inspection were carried out. At first sight it would appear that a detailed examination of the skeleton would be an important part of the identification process. Most people are familiar with television images of pathologists determining cause of death, age and even identity from dental records. Unfortunately all these activities are of limited use in a Great War context.

Bones reveal what is technically known as skeletal trauma, damage to the bones through injuries that may have led to the death of the subject. In a criminal context this is useful as the body is unlikely to suffer further trauma after death. On a battlefield the reverse is true. Bodies are frequently hit by further bullets or shell fragments, or even blown apart while lying unburied after death. It is therefore not possible to say whether an injury was part of the process leading to death, or simply sustained afterwards. Also knowing that the victim was shot in the head, for example, is not a good clue to identity as many causes of death were common to many soldiers. As far as identity goes it's a poor place to start. Skeletal evidence can be useful, however, if an identity has been postulated on the basis of other information. If, for example, the soldier put forward as a possible ID *was* shot in the head, negative evidence in the form of an intact skull might rule him out. Some basic data can also

Belgian pathologists at work on the initial clean of skeletal remains found at Bixschoote near Ypres, under the ever-watchful gaze of the television cameras. (*DRK*)

be useful. Height can be calculated for an individual using either the complete skeleton or the femur (thigh bone), so checking the skeletal height against that given in the service record can be used to rule a candidate in or out. However, starting with only height data is not typically helpful as many men shared the same stature.

Theoretically one form of skeletal trauma which might be useful is that of *healed* injuries. If our man broke his leg the year before he was killed and then returned to duty this might show on his skeleton and be comparable with his service record, but it relies not only on a particular set of events befalling the individual but also all those events being recorded in surviving documents. So far we have not been that lucky. Along with healed injuries, bones can also reveal occupational and lifestyle information. Some diseases such as arthritis and social conditions such as vitamin deficiencies or poor diet can also be identified. Unfortunately the demographics of the armies mean that the population (as any group of skeletons is described) of remains is dominated by fit men in their teens and twenties who are less likely to show significant signs of debility. Interesting work has been done on medieval skeletons to show that certain activities, in particular archery practice, can result in skeletal deformation. It has been suggested that more modern civilian occupations like mining might also leave similar traces, but this has not been firmly proven. The problem is that this kind of analysis relies on thousands of bones to produce statistically good results. The population of excavated fallen soldiers is simply not that large, and as most have quite properly been reburied, their bones are not available for analysis.

The team is also often asked whether we use DNA as a means of identification. Again television programmes have led to the perception that a DNA sample can be taken from human tissue and an identity revealed. The problem with the DNA of a fallen soldier is that while it might be relatively easy to produce a profile, there is no data against which to check it. It is possible that mitochondrial DNA patterns, preserved in the genes of a soldier's female relatives, could be used to confirm an identity, but again this would rely on the identity first being provisionally established by some other means so as to know whose relatives to test. Once again the problem of reburial also arises. Is it ethical to retain a bone sample from a set of remains and rebury the rest, just in case an identity is postulated in the future? At the time of writing these issues are becoming a topic of increasing debate but no firm decisions have been made, and certainly no funds have been made available to maintain such a store.

The work of the pathologist is certainly useful, and can serve as a cross-reference for other forms of identification evidence, but it is seldom the most important factor. Typically it is the archaeological conservators working in the laboratory who produce the key evidence. While some objects such as buttons are relatively robust, almost all other forms of artefactual identification evidence are extremely fragile. These can consist of paper items, pieces of embroidered cloth from uniforms, stamped leather or even badly corroded metal objects (including identification discs). Very little information can be gained from these kinds of items in the field, and over-zealous scraping of an object with a muddy trowel can all too easily destroy vital evidence. The excavators therefore have to be very patient and painstaking in their digging and recording, and equally patient in awaiting the lab results. The excitement of finding a key piece of evidence such as a book or wallet is balanced by frustration as the object is carefully packaged up, unopened and still covered with mud, and sent away for analysis.

The NML team has been very lucky in gaining the support of the conservation laboratories of the Institute of Archaeology at University College, London. Here objects can be examined using a battery of modern investigative techniques, from X-rays to specialist cleaning and preservation. However, as on the dig site, many of the best results come from sheer dogged patience as the conservators spend hours carefully picking away at the encrustations of rust and mud to reveal inscriptions or embroidery, or delicately peeling open pages of papers. Some of their more spectacular results include the name and address that Jakob Hönes had scratched into the back of his identification disc, revealed from under layers of corrosion, or the pages of bank books or soldiers' pay books revealed from what previously appeared to be no more than muddy lumps. Sadly not every carefully bagged muddy lump actually contains such 'treasure'; some are simply that – mud. A sealed cigarette tin was recovered from the dig at Vimy. This could have contained anything from actual cigarettes to a soldier's personal effects, so rather than open it on site the tin was sent off to UCL. After X-raying it was carefully prised open in the lab to reveal a dense packing of nothing but Vimy clay. The libellous e-mails that followed between the conservators and the excavators reveal the healthy rivalry which exists between different branches of the archaeological profession!

At the end of the process the team is confronted with a series of pieces of information. This includes site information, such as the location and

Conservators Christie and Dominica hard at work in the laboratories of the Institute of Archaeology. It is the painstaking work of the conservators which often produces the most spectacular results for the team. (*UCL*)

positioning of the body, pathological information on age and height, and possible trauma, and conserved artefacts revealing regimental details or more personal data. Inevitably this data will be partial, random and in some cases apparently contradictory. Where more than one individual is involved the situation can be even more complicated. Imagine taking three or more jigsaw puzzles, mixing up all the pieces in a bag, then taking out one or two handfuls of pieces. Sometimes the complete picture can be very hard to see.

This is where the third element of our team comes into play. NML is fortunate in having members who are experts in the documentation of the war: the personal records, regimental histories and casualty lists of both sides in the conflict. It is their job to make sense of the jumble of incomplete facts presented to them. How well they do this is highlighted in the next chapter. Success is by no means guaranteed, and luck plays a large part, but again, as on site or in the lab, much of it is down to boring hard work, going through lists in dusty archives looking for that one vital bit of data. Sometimes it is the apparent contradictions in the data which prove most rewarding. For example, in the case of Albert Thielecke, a soldier was found in a Württemberg regiment from Stuttgart, whose bank account was apparently held in Halberstadt in Saxony, on the other side of Germany. Why would a soldier have his account based so far away? (If indeed it was his.) The answer lay in his moving home between being called-up for Military Service and re-enlisting several years later. In many ways a bank account in Stuttgart would have been much more commonplace and thus less helpful in confirming the identity. As the next chapter will show, often any one piece of data will lead to a selection of individual names, and it is the comparison of each of these names against all the various bits of information available that is the key to success.

Earlier chapters of this book have shown that the excavation of Great War battlefields is not simply about the recovery of the dead. After all, the story of the war is also the story of the nine out of ten men (about 89 per cent of the BEF at least) who survived and went home. None the less the dead play a significant part, and their presence on the excavated sites has captured the interest and imagination of both visitors and television audiences, and has profoundly affected all the team members. Despite the fact that the uncovering of remains engenders an enormous amount of work for all concerned (almost all of which is undertaken voluntarily outside the budgets of the various projects), it leaves a sense of great satisfaction among all those involved. All armies no matter how large are ultimately made up of individual soldiers, not much different from you and me. The stories of four of those individuals follow in the next chapter.

Chapter 6

Four Stories

TEAMWORK

This final chapter tells the stories of the discovery of some of the soldiers' remains uncovered by the team. It also tells the individual stories of the lives of those men, as far as it has been possible to reconstruct them. The sample is random, guided by the chance coincidences of excavation; we did not choose them. If anything they chose us. That all three of the named individuals were German is a coincidence, but as far as the team was concerned it was irrelevant as they stand for *all* the participants in the conflict. As a sample of the participants in the war these men are not typical in that all of them were killed (otherwise we would not have been able to discover them archaeologically), but it is hoped that their experience reflects that of many of their comrades and opponents.

Perhaps more than any of the other chapters in the book, this one was a team effort. Much of the narrative which follows has been constructed, sometimes verbatim, from the research reports and contributions of different team members, so specific acknowledgement is required. The excavations in question were directed by David Kenyon, Martin Brown and Jon Price. The excavation of the human remains and the initial processing of the associated artefacts was supervised by Luke Barber. Dean Sully and Renata Peters at UCL then oversaw the laboratory analysis of some of these objects. The resulting data fragments went on to Alastair Fraser in the UK and Judy Ruzlo in Canada, who coordinated the efforts of a documentary research team which included Steve Roberts in the UK, Ralph Whitehead in the USA, and Volker Hartmann and Alexander Brunotte in Germany. In all cases the initial excavations were paid for with television money (from the BBC and YAP films), but the identification research typically continued long after the relevant programmes had been broadcast and any available budget expended. The team was working therefore for no more reward than the satisfaction of seeing it through, and sheer curiosity as to where it would lead. For at least one soldier the case remains open, as no identification has yet been forthcoming, so in that sense the work continues. (Anyone who is expert on the pre-war garrison of the Channel Islands is urged to contact us!)

WEHRMANN JAKOB HÖNES

In October 2003 the BBC in the UK produced a television documentary telling the story of the English war poet Wilfred Owen. In his letters to his mother Owen described his terrible experiences in a dug-out during the Somme battles of early 1917, experiences which inspired some of his most famous poetry. As part of the programme, the BBC commissioned the No-Man's-Land team to look for Owen's dug-out. As a result an archaeological excavation was carried out in the area where the poet was known to have been serving in those terrible days of February 1917. His post was actually in a recently captured portion of the German front line near the village of Serre, a salient in the German line known as the 'Heidenkopf'. In the event no dug-out was found, but the excavation revealed the remains of three soldiers killed in the fighting in that area.

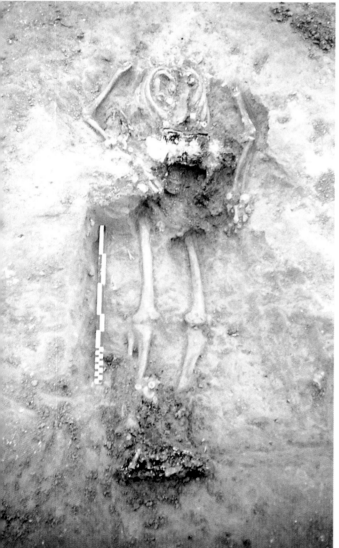

On the second day on site the team identified several human bones on the surface of the excavation area (plough soil had previously been removed by mechanical digger). Careful excavation around the bones revealed a male skeleton, complete apart from the skull, which had been destroyed by

The remains of Jakob Hönes. The full ammunition pouches are clearly visible, along with the arrangement of the buttons. No skull was present due to plough damage. (*DRK*)

eighty years of agricultural activity over the site. The remainder of the body had been protected as it was lying in a shallow shell hole. In addition to the bones, a range of German military equipment was found still in position around the skeleton. Cloth items had almost entirely disappeared, but leather and metal objects survived.

The skeleton was found to be wearing German leather jackboots, and around the waist was a full set of belt equipment of the obsolete 1895 pattern. The ammunition pouches were full, indeed an extra charger of rounds had been forced into each pouch in addition to the nine the pouches were designed for. A torch was also found, but the water-bottle and entrenching tool were missing. This man had clearly been prepared for some stiff fighting, but had died before he had the chance to use any of his ammunition. It was not uncommon for German soldiers defending their trench lines to concentrate on weapons and ammunition and dispense with the rest of their heavy field equipment. No weapons were found. In his bread bag were a mirror and comb, and what was apparently a nail-cleaner, perhaps suggesting a man concerned with his appearance.

Each item was carefully excavated and its location on the skeleton recorded. Some items were cleaned and examined on site, while other fragile objects were packed up and sent to the conservation laboratory at UCL for detailed preservation and examination. Once this archaeological work was complete, the results were passed to Alastair Fraser, and he began the detective work, which led from these objects to the identification of an individual soldier. Much of what follows is a summary of his more detailed report.

The first thing was to determine which units had been in the area. The early pattern of much of the equipment pointed to a casualty of 1915 or 1916, and he was clearly a German. During this period the 'Heidenkopf' had been garrisoned by the German army's 26th Reserve Division, 12th Division, 52nd Division, and 1st and 2nd Garde Infanterie Divisions. None of the distinctive uniform decoration of Garde troops was present, but more importantly, the buttons on the casualty's tunic suggested an M1910 Waffenrock tunic, with 'Swedish' pattern cuffs (two buttons aligned horizontally rather than vertically). Such cuffs were worn by many Württemberg regiments, but by only one which had served in the site area, namely the 121st Reserve Infanterie Regiment of the 26th Reserve Division. Examination of photographs in the relevant regimental history showed these distinctive buttons. (Alastair collects these histories, mostly by purchase via the internet, and has a significant collection.) The belt equipment was also of the obsolete M1895 pattern, widely issued to reserve regiments. Curiously the belt buckle was a Bavarian pattern, but this could have been acquired as an unofficial replacement for a broken item.

The casualty had in his pocket the decorated glass lid of a shoe cream or dubbin pot from the E. Breuninger department store in Stuttgart. A visit by team member Martin Brown to the store confirmed this; indeed, it is a product they still sell, albeit in different packaging. Also, and crucially, a badly corroded partial identity disc of early pattern was discovered. These early discs did not carry the soldier's name but included his regiment and his company and, crucially, the individual soldier's number on the company roll. After conservation at UCL, several letters could be discerned on the disc: 'Res R. No.', '7 Ko . . .' and 'No. 2'. In addition, a series of letters had been scratched unofficially on the back of the disc. These were very difficult to read, but Alastair, in concert with Volker Hartmann, a German member of the team, was able to read 'Mün . . . ', 'Hines' and 'Jak . . .', suggesting a possible name 'Jak[ob] Hines'. The problem with this is that 'Hines' is not a common German surname.

At this point it was possible to suggest that the casualty was 'Jakob Hines' of No. 7 Company of a reserve

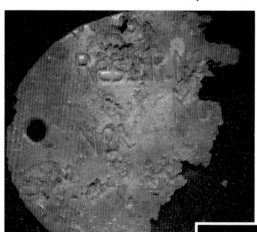

The identification tag belonging to Jakob Hönes, showing the incomplete printed numbers on the front . . .

regiment. Consultation of the regimental history of the 121st Reserve Regiment showed that No. 7 Company of the regiment had been attacked by the French in the 'Heidenkopf' in June 1915, and had taken casualties. By a great piece of luck, Alastair was able to contact Ralph Whitehead, in Fayetteville, New York, via the internet. Ralph is a researcher who has spent many years researching the casualty lists of the 14th Reserve Korps of the German army, a formation which included the 121st Reserve Regiment. He was able to supply a copy of the regimental casualty lists, and these showed that on 13 June 1915 Jakob Hönes of No. 7 Company, 121st Reserve Infantry Regiment, had been killed in the 'Heidenkopf' area. Re-examination of the identity tag suggested that the character originally interpreted as an 'i' could just as easily be an 'ö'. Ralph was also able to show that Hönes was originally from the village of Münchingen, near Stuttgart, explaining the 'Mün . . .' on the tag. Hönes was shown in the casualty list as 'killed' but not as 'missing',

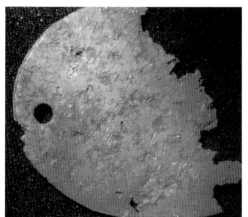

suggesting either that someone had seen him fall, or that he had been given a temporary burial. The presence of groundsheet eyelets around the body suggested that the latter may have been the case, but the grave location may have been lost when the position fell to the British in November 1916.

Contact was made with the town archives of Korntal-

. . . and the scratched information on the reverse giving Jakob's name and part of his home town. (*UCL*)

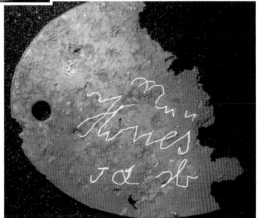

Münchingen, and subsequently with the Hönes family. Astonishingly, Jakob's son Ernst Christian was still alive, at the age of 93 (he would have been just 4 years old when his father left for the war), and although he died in March 2004 he lived long enough to learn of the rediscovery of his father after so many years. Through the family, and through research undertaken by Alexander Brunotte in the local archives, it is now possible to tell much of the story of Jakob's life and the events leading to his death.

Jakob Friedrich Hönes was born in Münchingen, a small agricultural village a few miles from Stuttgart, on 9 December 1880. He was the eldest of three boys (Jakob, Karl and Christian) and one girl (two more girls died in infancy) born to his father Georg Hönes. When their mother Christiane Sofie died, Georg remarried, producing Jakob's step-brother Wilhelm. Jakob attended the local elementary school (*Volksschule*) for the minimum statutory period, from the ages of 7 to 14, and then left to work as a farm labourer. His profession was recorded locally as either a farmer or a day labourer.

At the age of 20 he was called up and performed his initial military service with 121st Infanterie Regiment 'Alt Württemburg' between 1900 and 1902, before being transferred to the reserves, the Landwehr. After military service he returned to Münchingen and continued in casual work. He is recorded working both as a brick-maker in the local brickworks, and as a bricklayer, as well as in agricultural work. In 1908 Jakob married Marie Ansel, a woman from the nearby village of Hirschlanden. A photograph of the couple, probably taken at their wedding, shows Jakob in his Reservist's uniform, an expression of his pride in his military service but also more practically probably the smartest suit of clothes he owned. By the time of their marriage, Marie and Jakob already had a 7-year-old child, and the family grew steadily to a total of six children. In 1911 they were able to buy a house and a small plot of land of their own.

Jakob was recalled to the colours on 6 August 1914, and left for the front while Marie remained at home, pregnant with their last child, a daughter Luise, who would be born at Christmas 1914. He was posted on 3 September 1914 to No. 7 Company of the 121st Reserve Regiment and fought with them in the Vosges and at Nancy before moving to the Somme area in October 1914. He spent the winter of 1914/15 on the Somme, as his last child was born back in Münchingen. However, his youngest brother Christian was at home at that time convalescing from a wound and may have been able to visit the child. Christian joined

Jakob in No. 7 Company on 2 April 1915, and the two were able to serve together.

The regimental history records that on 10 June 1915 II Battalion (including No. 7 Company) moved up under fire from its billets at Miraumont to positions along the Serre to Mailly-Maillet road (later to become known as the 'Heidenkopf'). After several days of intermittently heavy French bombardment the position was assaulted on the morning of 13 June. The French attackers were able temporarily to capture the German front trenches but after much bitter fighting they were repulsed. The battalion suffered 314 casualties including their commander, Hauptman Nagel, and, as the casualty returns show, Wehrmann Jakob Hönes:

> List of casualties Nr. 226
>
> 13 June 1915, killed in action near Serre, shot by rifle bullet.
>
> Buried next to the lines, 1 km south of Serre near Albert in Northern France
>
> Certified by Friedrich von Raben
>
> (Captain and Company Commander)
>
> Courcelette, 18 June 1915

Family legend says that Christian was present at the death of his brother, who 'died in his arms', but this cannot be verified. Christian himself was to die only 13 months later on 24 July 1916 during the battle of the Somme; severely wounded near Beaumont by a shell, he died in the dressing station at Miraumont. Their step-brother Wilhelm was also killed at around the same time, at Hill 60 near Ypres. A series of three field postcards from Jakob to Marie survive from May 1915. Amid expressions of concern for the health of his large family, he commented, 'I reckon we have seen most of it', expressing the view that the war would soon be over. He signed off another:

> Meanwhile a kiss and greetings from your dear husband Jakob, dear Marie, and from your dear father, dear children Albert, Emma, Eugen, little Ernst, Sophie and Luise. Goodbye. Forget me not.

His war was to end within two months of those words. Marie carried on raising the children and married again in 1920, but was to suffer further loss as her new husband was captured on the Eastern Front in the Second World War, and died in a Soviet prison camp in 1947.

It was with some surprise that the archaeological team learned that before going up to the trenches Jakob had been billeted in Miraumont. As their usual accommodation in Auchonvillers was not available, the archaeologists had been living in a converted hayloft in a stable in Miraumont, thus unknowingly they had followed in the Hönes brothers' footsteps each morning as they made their journey to the excavation site. In August 2004 the funeral was held in Labry military cemetery, near Metz, of Wehrmann Jakob Hönes, in the presence of members of his family. By coincidence some Bundeswehr soldiers were also present in the cemetery, and were only too happy to provide an impromptu honour guard for his interment.

This postcard depicts Jakob (lying down at bottom left) and his colleagues of the 121st Reserve Regiment in Miraumont. Such group photo postcards were common in the German army. (*Walter Rapp*)

Subsequently in June 2006 more than twenty members of the extended Hönes family made the journey to France to see the site where Jakob had been found. They had suggested that a memorial marker be placed near the spot, as his remains had been taken to a German cemetery on the other side of France, no space being available in local sites. The NML

The unveiling of the three soldiers' memorial at Serre. *(Left to right)*: Alastair Fraser (researcher), Andrew Robertshaw, David Kenyon, Keith Maddison (sculptor), Steve Roberts (researcher), Volker Hartmann and Alexander Brunotte (German researchers), and Walter Rapp, grandson of Jakob. *(DRK)*

team members were very keen on this idea, but extended the project to include all three soldiers found during that dig. A small memorial was designed and created by team member Keith Maddison, a sculptor by profession (NML includes a pool of surprisingly varied talents), and the team clubbed together with the family to raise the funds. It was formally unveiled in the presence of television crews and journalists, as well as official delegations from the armed forces of the UK, France and Germany, during the family's June visit. The discovery also provoked interest in Germany beyond just the Hönes family and an exhibition was staged in Münchingen telling the story of Jakob as well as the wider story of the town's experience of the war. Ripples continue to extend from Jakob, as at the time of writing NML members are looking forward to a visit to Münchingen to attend the annual town festival – all because ninety-one years ago a soldier broke the regulations and scratched his name on his ID tag.

UNTEROFFIZIER ALBERT THIELECKE

Only a few metres from the remains of Jakob Hönes, a second skeleton was uncovered. Again the body was very close to the modern ground surface, immediately below the ploughed layer, lying on its left side with the legs slightly bent. When the remains were excavated German pattern jackboots were immediately apparent. Further excavation revealed a number of tunic and trouser buttons bearing the Prussian crown, lying in positions indicative that the body had been buried wearing a tunic. A belt was also present, but there were no ammunition pouches or other equipment. Most significant, however, were the contents of the tunic and trouser pockets, and of a canvas bread bag worn on the right hip. While

the bag and the garments had decayed entirely their contents were still *in situ*, giving the excavators an insight into the private world of this soldier.

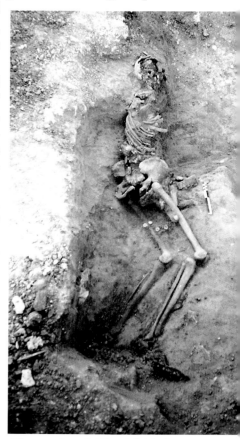

Around the right hip, thus in the bag or right pocket, were found a silver nickel floral-decorated fob watch (stopped at ten past six), a harmonica, a cut-throat razor, a penknife, a set of keys and the remains of a pipe and tobacco wrapped in newspaper. There was also a purse containing twenty-seven German coins of small denomination; the latest date identified on these was 1915. Somewhat mysteriously, a worked flint tool, dating from the Late Neolithic period, was also present in the bag. The Somme is a chalk area and so flint is relatively commonplace. Anyone with an expert eye can pick up worked prehistoric tools from the surrounding fields, but it was clear from the position of this flake that it was not merely lying adjacent to the body but had been *in* the bag. This soldier was clearly interested enough to both recognise and keep a worked flint – had we inadvertently excavated a fellow archaeologist?

The remains of Albert Thielecke, as uncovered in the 'Heidenkopf' at Serre. Fragments of his boots are clearly visible in the foreground. (*DRK*)

The contents of Albert Thielecke's bread bag. His watch and harmonica are clearly visible, as well as a prehistoric worked flint tool – did he have an interest in archaeology? (*DRK*)

The soil surrounding both the bag and the lower portion of the body was thick with the pupa cases of blowflies. In some areas these formed a solid black crust in the soil. Clearly the body and the remaining rations in the bread bag had lain exposed on the surface for long enough to be thoroughly infested with maggots. Some groundsheet eyelets were present, suggesting the body might have been carried or wrapped in a sheet, but if so any burial cannot have taken place immediately after death as the flies had had enough time to get to work. This provided grim evidence of conditions in the trenches at that time (as well as an indication that the death may well have occurred during warm weather in the summer).

As far as identifying this soldier was concerned, the key items were found when the bones were lifted from the soil. Under the pelvis, and probably originally in the left-hand pocket of the tunic, was a soggy lump identified as a pocket book or bundle of papers. This was immediately dispatched to the lab for conservation and examination. The work in the conservation laboratory at UCL was complex and painstaking. The book proved to be from a bank and was an indication of status and wealth as might be expected for a senior NCO in the

German army. However, the bank in question was in Halberstadt, a town in Saxony, about 530km away from Stuttgart. In theory an officer in a Württemberg regiment would have been living in that state and would not be from another part of Germany. Ralph Whitehead checked up on the German 'Verlustlisten' (lists of casualties) for the 121st Reserve Regiment and found that Albert Thielecke was a likely candidate as he had moved from Saxony to Württemberg before the war began and had served briefly in the 122nd Regiment. The company roll of 7/RIR 121, which was checked by Alexander Brunotte in Stuttgart, confirmed this assumption. It was also stated there that Albert was killed by a 'Gewehrgeschoss' (rifle bullet) on 11 June 1915. The body measurements given in the peacetime company roll of 3/Füsilierregiment 122 also corresponded to the size of the bones found at Serre, suggesting we had the right man.

Having achieved a provisional identification for the remains, the team had a stroke of good luck. The *Stuttgarter Zeitung* newspaper ran an article about the planned memorial for Jakob, Albert and the unknown British soldier. At that time a young woman called Susanna Thielecke, who had been living in Stuttgart for a few years, was directing rehearsals of an English-speaking drama group that was going to perform G.B. Shaw's *O'Flaherty VC* along with recitals of war poems and letters by Wilfred Owen and others at a small theatre in Stuttgart-Bad Cannstatt. An American actor passed the article from the *Stuttgarter Zeitung* on to her because the name 'Thielecke' cropped up in it. In due course Susanna Thielecke rang Alexander Brunotte at the Münchingen archives and told him that she might possibly be related to Albert since her family had roots at Halberstadt, although she didn't know any genealogical details. Alexander was referred to her father Karl, a retired teacher in Regensburg, who, she said, had all the time in the world to do the necessary research – and that is precisely what he did. Most of what follows is based on research carried out by Karl Thielecke into his own family history.

Albert Thielecke was born on 31 December 1888 in Halberstadt, in the Magdeburg district of the province of Saxony, part of what was then the Kingdom of Prussia. His parents were August Thielecke, a foreman carpenter, and his wife Maria (née Sachs). They lived in a half-timbered house in Kuehlinger Strasse where Albert was born.

There were three children: Albert's sister Minna, who was ten years his senior, and a brother August, who was just less than two years older than Albert. The young Albert probably joined the building trade along with

The house in Kuehlinger Strasse in Halberstadt where Albert Thielecke was born. This is the house which subsequently burnt down during bombing in 1945, and from which the mystery photograph was rescued. (*Karl Thielecke*)

his father, as his profession is variously recorded as *Polsterer und Dekorateur* (upholsterer and painter-decorator) or *Tapezierer* (decorator).

In October 1910, at the age of 22, Albert began his military career. He joined the 7th Company of Infantry Regiment 27 'Prinz Louis Ferdinand von Preußen' (2. Magdeburger) at Halberstadt, as a volunteer for two years. He may have moved away from home for a while before returning to Halberstadt to enlist, as according to the company roll he had lived in Bad Oeynhausen (Westfalia) before he entered the army. At that time Musketeer Thielecke was 1.65m tall (approximately 5ft 6ins), his weight was 57kg (nearly 9 stone), and his chest measurement 80/89cm (32/36ins). Probably his hearing was slightly hampered as both of his eardrums were described as 'opaque'. He was fair-haired and sported a moustache.

Military life seems to have suited Albert. In 1912 he was awarded the *Schützenabzeichen* (rifleman's badge) for the high standard of his shooting. At any rate he decided to remain in the army. He was discharged to the reserves two weeks before the end of his two-year enlistment on 16 September 1912, presumably in order to allow him some leave before on 1 October he joined the 3rd Company of Infantry Regiment ('Füsilierregiment') 122 'Kaiser Franz Joseph von Österreich' (4. Württembergisches) in Heilbronn as a so-called *Kapitulant* – the term used for someone who re-enlisted after his military service had ended in order to become an 'Unteroffizier' (non-commissioned officer). Albert Thielecke agreed to serve as a *Kapitulant* for two years from 1 October 1912 until the end of September 1914. Why he chose to do this in Heilbronn, hundreds of kilometres away from Halberstadt, is unknown but he may have had to look further afield for a suitable vacancy.

In the course of his training as a non-commissioned officer Thielecke had to attend school-lessons (*Kapitulanten-Unterricht*). Among the surviving documents in the Stuttgart archives today is a school report for Unteroffizier Thielecke, dating from 14 April 1913. He was evidently an adequate student but not what you could call an excellent pupil. His marks were:

German: sufficient (*hinreichend*)

Maths: sufficient

Writing: sufficient

Overall performance: sufficient

Thielecke was promoted to the rank of Gefreiter (lance corporal) almost immediately on 3 October 1912 and Unteroffizier (non-commissioned officer) shortly after in December of that year.

With the outbreak of war in 1914 Albert was transferred away from IR 122. He joined the 7th Company of the 121st Reserve Infantry Regiment (Jakob Hönes's regiment) with which he stayed until his death in 1915. He and Jakob must have known each other, since they were in the same company, but there is no evidence that they were friends; also Albert was an NCO and Jakob a private. From August until the end of September 1914 the company was involved in fighting in the Vosges mountains in eastern France before transferring to the Somme front. There Albert was placed in command of the company baggage wagon, and received the Iron Cross Second Class. It is possible that the award was for conspicuous service in the Vosges, and perhaps the cushy job on the wagon may have been a more informal but practical recognition of his achievements.

Unteroffizier Albert Thielecke was killed at Serre on 11 June 1915 (two days before Jakob). His death notice in the company roll reads:

List of casualties Nr. 404

11 June 1915, fallen near Serre at 7 a.m. Shot in his head by rifle bullet.

Buried next to the lines, 1 km south of Serre near Albert in Northern France

Certified by Friedrich von Raben

(Captain and Company Commander)

In the line near Thiepval, 22 June 1915

That he was buried immediately behind the trenches is demonstrated by where he was found. It is difficult to say how much ceremony would

have accompanied his burial. So close was the location to the French lines that it is likely to have been a hurried night-time affair with possibly only his immediate company members pausing briefly over him before returning to the safety of the trench. He was shot in the head, but was buried still wearing his soft *mutze* cap. The national cockade from the front of this cap was one of the

August Thielecke's treasured picture, which was recovered from the burning house. Does it depict Albert? (*Karl Thielecke*)

first items recovered when his remains were found. Steel helmets were not available in the German army until February 1916 and did not appear on the Somme front until the autumn of that year.

Albert's brother August (the elder by 22 months) also did his initial military service in Infanterie-Regiment No. 27 in Halberstadt. On 4 August 1914, possibly in response to his imminent departure for the war, he married his fiancée Helene, a lodger in the Thielecke family home. August survived nearly five years of war with IR 27, and when he returned had risen to the rank of Feldwebel (Company Sergeant-Major). As a member of the regular army, he had a claim to employment in the civil service and ended up in the Post Office. August and Helene had a son, christened Albert, possibly in memory of the lost younger brother, but August must have kept his feelings under wraps as none of the living members of the Thielecke family had ever heard of an older uncle Albert.

There is, however, a photo in their possession which can be traced back to the personal effects of August Thielecke. It must have been very dear to him. It is charred round the edges from the fire which destroyed the family home in Kuehlinger Strasse after the city of Halberstadt was bombed by the RAF on 8 April 1945, so August must have gone to considerable trouble to salvage this picture from the burning house. The picture shows a proud young soldier in battle dress. The edging of his collar indicates that he was an NCO. He carries a sabre and a silver tassel (called a 'portepee'), which was reserved for senior NCOs who were able to act as officers. So this young gentleman must have been either a Vizefeldwebel or even a Feldwebel, but he is not August. His headdress is a *Pickelhaube* still and not a steel helmet, also he is wearing jackboots and not gaiters, so the picture must have been taken in the first half of the war. Is this young man Albert Thielecke?

GEFREITER LEOPOLD ROTHÄRMEL

In the spring of 2005 the NML team carried out a week of excavations at Auchy les Mines in northern France. This site was selected as it formed part of the battlefield of Loos. In particular it was the site of the German Hohenzollern Redoubt, the scene of vicious fighting and mining in 1915–16. Several large mine craters survived on the site un-backfilled, and it was hoped that these could be explored as part of one of the *Trench Detectives* series.

All went well until the second-last day of the project. On the Friday afternoon two team members were tasked with examining something possibly thought to be a dug-out entrance: a chalk-filled feature approximately 1.5m square, shored with timber on its west side. However, at a depth of approximately 1.5m below the modern surface two human skulls were uncovered. This find was initially interpreted as two individuals buried within the entrance to a deep dug-out. The two people allocated the job were both team members without much archaeological experience, so the discovery of human remains was quite a shock (although not unexpected, it is none the less always a powerful moment). For the project management it provided a difficult technical problem. The skulls were deeply buried, and if they were in a dug-out entrance then their bodies could be lying at an angle descending even more deeply into the ground. Also the team had only one more full day on site. None the less it was determined that we were ethically obliged, having disturbed them, to attempt to recover these two individuals as completely as possible.

Due to pressure of time, the area surrounding the two skulls was reduced using a mechanical excavator. This left a large square area about 8m across and 1.5m deep with the skulls in the centre. Hand-digging was then begun to reveal the remains themselves. By the time the machine had finished it was growing dark on the Friday night and the team was due to finish the dig on Saturday. The site had also been visited by looters earlier in the week and no one wanted to risk leaving the bodies, despite the presence of hired local security. The result was a shift system. Floodlights were set up, and half the team was sent away to rest and return in the morning, while the other half set about digging through the night. It was also raining so a plastic tent had to be improvised over the hole, not for our benefit but because mud would quickly render the excavation impossible. It was a night of cold, rain and snatched sleep as the team members worked in pairs on the remains – a dark grim night which no one present will ever forget.

Rather than exposing the entrance to a dug-out, it became apparent that the skulls were the uppermost of a series of at least five sets of human remains, contained within a linear cut, possibly a disused trench. Several of the bodies appeared to have been placed there deliberately, and were thus likely to be part of a mass burial. It was determined that the burials were placed within a trench used in October 1915 as an impromptu grave. This was then buried under a layer of mine upcast possibly from early 1916. Subsequently the entrance to a deep dug-out was begun, but this was abandoned when the men digging it encountered the human remains below.

Four complete articulated individuals were removed from the trench. Significant quantities of German clothing and military equipment were recovered, as well as personal items associated with these individuals (there was also a significant amount of British equipment mixed with them). The majority of the items associated with these individuals went to the UK for cleaning and analysis. On removal of the four uppermost casualties, there were indications that further human remains were present below and to the side, and it was suspected that the trench was filled for some distance along its length with a large number of bodies. Unfortunately, due to pressure of time, the team was not able to continue working (we had been on site continuously in shifts for over 40 hours at that point). A decision was therefore taken to mark and backfill the site, with a view to returning when resources and time became available in the future. There is clear historical and anecdotal evidence supporting the substantial loss of life in the area of the Hohenzollern. Eyewitness accounts record trenches choked with dead and wounded, and it is certainly possible that this is what was partially uncovered here (although there is evidence that at least some of the burials were deliberate).

Artefacts were found associated with each of the sets of remains, but our attention quickly focused on items that were found between the second and third bodies down (skeletons 12 and 13 in the site records). These included the remains of several possible books and a tunic with clear buttons and regimental markings. The uniform remains recovered included an embroidered shoulder tab showing a figure '16' and some Bavarian

Cloth shoulder strap from a German tunic showing the embroidered '16' of the 16th Bavarian Reserve Infantry Regiment. This was the key to unlocking the identity of Leopold Rothärmel. (*UCL*)

buttons, indicating a Bavarian regiment, either the 16th Bavarian Infantry Regiment or the 16th Bavarian Reserve Infantry Regiment. Records indicated that the 16th BIR had not been present in the Hohenzollern Redoubt, leaving the 16th RIR as the most probable unit. A review of the casualty records for the period 3–8 October when that unit was in the trenches near Auchy indicates that thirty-three members of this regiment were killed in action or died from wounds suffered during this period. Of these, seventeen have no known burial location.

Of the documents recovered with the bodies, some portions remained legible and were later restored. One document was a *Soldbuch*, an individual soldier's pay book and service record, often used as his identity document. On one page several dates could still be made out, including 16 April 1915; on another there was also a section headed 'depot 6. Bayer'. Possibly the strongest evidence came from a partially preserved postcard mailed in München (Munich) that contained the words 'Gefreiter Leopold Rothä . . .' in the address section. This postcard matches only one of the missing men from the 9th Company by

Pages of *Alte und Neue Soldaten-lieder*, the songbook which not only helped to identify Leopold Rothärmel, but also gave a poignant glimpse of his character and talents as a musician. (*UCL*)

rank, first name and a good portion of the family name: Gefreiter Leopold Rothärmel. A military songbook was also recovered.

Based on this evidence it was concluded that one of the sets of remains recovered in February 2005 was that of Gefreiter Leopold Rothärmel. Unfortunately the tunics were between the bodies rather than actually worn, and the books and documents, while lying very close to two of the skeletons, could not be associated with one of them in particular. It is likely, on the basis of the presence of the documentary material between Bodies 12 and 13, that he is one of those two. Skeletal damage to the head of body 12, suggesting a possible alternative cause of death, may help to rule out that skeleton, thus it is probable that body 13 is that of Gefreiter Rothärmel. However, the team could not be certain. Normal policy, owing to the lack of space for new burials in the few available German cemeteries, is that named individuals are buried two at a time in discrete graves and unnamed bodies go into a large mass grave. The team did not want to risk placing a name over the wrong grave, so in this instance all four men were placed in a single individual grave, with a marker to indicate that Rothärmel and three other men were buried there. He's almost certainly in there, we just don't know which one he is.

The archives in Munich revealed that Leopold Rothärmel was born on 20 October 1892 in Munich, Bavaria. He was one of two sons and four daughters of Leopold and Emma Rothärmel. He was the second youngest and his brother Otto was the youngest. (Otto, too, was to serve in the war, after he was enlisted in the 4 Bavarian RIR.) Their father, Leopold senior, was a registered installer of water and gas pipes. The family also ran a small corner shop, with the mother as the shopkeeper. The family appeared to move every couple of years, always to rental apartments and always in the centre of Munich. The last known address for the family was Salvatorstrasse 4/2, which they moved into in July 1915. The last address where Leopold junior lived with his family just prior to enlistment was at Westenriederstrasse 32/3. Unfortunately these premises were bombed in the Second World War and no longer exist.

Leopold studied music at school in Munich and went on to become a 'concertmeister' – a position equivalent to a First Violin or Leader of an orchestra. He had also completed his military service prior to August 1914. As a musician, his work would have been somewhat itinerant. He spent some time in Augsburg (13 January–26 June 1912), and was registered in Berlin in April 1914. On 25 February 1915 Reservist Rothärmel was recalled to the army and was sent to the Infanterie Leibregiment Rekruten Depot III located at the Türkenkaserne in

Munich. On 17 March 1915 he was assigned to the 1st Field Company. On 16 April he was sent to the depot of the 6th Bavarian Reserve Division in Santes. The date '16.4.1915' and 'depot 6. Bayer' correspond with the information recovered from the *Soldbuch*.

On 17 May 1915 Rothärmel was assigned to the 9th Company, 16th Bavarian RIR. He was involved in fighting in the battles at La Bassée and Arras between 17 May and 23 July 1915, and on 5 July he was awarded the Iron Cross Second Class. Two days later he was promoted to the rank of Gefreiter. Part of an Iron Cross ribbon was identified on one of the excavated tunics. This decoration was typically worn on the uniform as a ribbon looped around one of the button-holes on the front of the tunic. Normally this would be sewn into position, and the actual Iron Cross itself kept separate, often sent home for safe-keeping. The ribbon found in the excavation had been temporarily attached with a safety-pin, suggesting its wearer had yet to get around to sewing it on properly.

The regimental history of the 16th Bavarian RIR also records that around this time there was 'an outbreak of musicality' in No. 9 Company. Gefreiter Rothärmel was involved in forming the music section of a choir within the ranks of the company in August 1915. This corresponds with his civilian occupation, and explains the presence of a songbook among his effects.

Leopold's unit was on trench duty from 24 July until 24 September 1915. The 9/16th Bavarian RIR was sent to the Hohenzollern Redoubt on 3 October 1915 as reinforcements along with the 12th and 16th companies from the 16th Bavarian RIR and two companies from the 17th Bavarian RIR. No. 9 Company participated in an attack against an enemy-occupied trench, called the *Popp Graben*, in the Hohenzollern Redoubt, along with the 10/17th Bavarian RIR. Company records show that Gefreiter Rothärmel participated in this attack. The attack began at 7 a.m. and within 25 minutes the trench was taken. Both companies came under heavy artillery fire for the remainder of the day.

The records of the 9/16th Bavarian RIR also include a report, signed by Isidor Neher, Leutnant der Infanterie and Company Commander of the 9/16th RIR, at Santes on 11 October 1915, indicating that on 3 October 1915 Gefreiter Rothärmel was killed at Auchy from a gunshot wound to the abdomen. His place of burial was not known. From the description it seems likely that he was killed during the 25-minute assault against the British defenders of the *Popp Graben*. There was no further infantry fighting on this date, but the two Bavarian companies were subjected to concentrated shrapnel fire for the rest of the day.

Tunic cloth and
iron cross

<26>   [12]

The ribbon of an Iron Cross, attached with a safety-pin to the button hole of a tunic, possibly that awarded to Leopold Rothärmel. The ribbon is recognisable by the broad central stripe and two narrow side stripes. (*UCL*)

During the excavations it was noted that the lower three bodies uncovered were probably Bavarians and most probably belonged to the 16th Bavarian RIR. The positioning of the remains suggested that they were buried in a careful manner. By contrast the top two bodies appeared to be mixed in with British equipment and seemed to indicate a more hasty burial, judging by the posture of the bodies. The top two were also associated with uniform markings showing a Prussian unit.

The 16th Bavarian RIR was the only Bavarian unit in this portion of the trench, and the same can be said for the subsequent troops, No. 2 Company, 55th RIR from the 2nd Guard Reserve Division, who were probably the only Prussians to occupy this area. This unit relieved the Bavarians, but a short time later was driven out of the trench leaving behind a large number of dead. Considering their sequence in the grave it is possible that the top bodies were members of the latter regiment who abandoned the redoubt under the heavy fire that preceded the British counter-attack.

Two of the uppermost bodies from the Hohenzollern Redoubt. Note the raised elbows resulting from the bodies possibly being carried by the arms and casually dumped, in contrast to the more formally laid out lower burials. (*LB*)

This has led to speculation that Leopold and his two Bavarian companions were buried carefully by their comrades, while the position was in German hands. The top two possible Prussians were buried later by the British after their successful attack and capture of the trench. The area was to remain British for some time to come so there were no other German units in this location. There was not enough to determine the identity of the other bodies but the evidence does point strongly to these two units, one Bavarian and one Prussian.

By the time of Leopold's death, his brother Otto was already dead, killed six months before on 4 April 1915 in the Wood of Ailly, to the south on part of the Somme battlefield. His place of burial also remains unknown. No more is known of the Rothärmel family. The last known address in Munich was destroyed by Allied bombing during the Second World War, and no living relatives have been traced or come forward. There is also the suggestion that the family name was Jewish and that any surviving family may have suffered at the hands of the Nazis, which is ironic given that Corporal Adolf Hitler was serving with the 16th Bavarian RIR at the same time as Leopold.

A SOLDIER OF THE KINGS OWN

The stories told so far are the successes in terms of identification, but there is not always so much to go on. In the case of Jakob the team was lucky to find an ID tag, and even luckier that the owner had unofficially modified it. Albert and Leopold left us documents by which to trace them. The other three Germans found at Loos were not associated with any items which allowed their identification, and so had to be reburied as unknown. Indeed, as probable Prussians, the search would have been difficult as the Prussian Military Archive was completely destroyed by the RAF in 1945. The same, sadly, was true of the third body found on the Serre excavation in 2003.

As has been described earlier in this book, the trenches of the 'Heidenkopf' were rapidly backfilled on 1 July 1916 by spoil from a German defensive mine, blown as the British were attacking on that fateful day. When a portion of that trench was excavated, a third set of

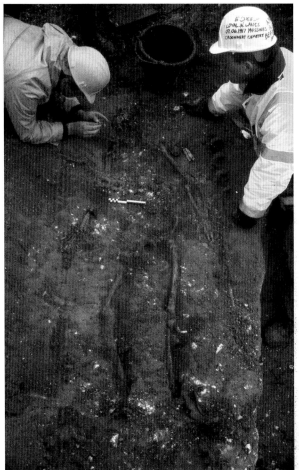

remains was found lying on top of the chalk fill of the trench. The skeleton was more or less complete, and was found lying outstretched on its back. Associated equipment suggested it was a British soldier. As in the other cases, fabric items had decayed more or less completely, but the various buttons and buckles from the tunic and trousers survived, as well as the boots, and a variety of other more decay-resistant objects.

The remains of a soldier of the Kings Own under excavation at Serre. This man's identity remains unknown but he had perhaps the grandest funeral of all the dead uncovered by the team. (*DRK*)

Examination of the skeleton itself revealed massive damage to the facial area of the skull, but it was impossible to say whether this had been incurred pre- or post-mortem. A large exit hole in the rear of the skull suggested that the damage was a 'through and through' injury, which possibly argues for it being the cause of death, rather than later plough damage for example. The right femur (thigh bone) was broken, and demonstrated the classic foreshortening of the leg which occurs with this injury as the two broken ends of the bone overlap, pulled together by the spasming thigh muscle. This too could have been a fatal injury as damage to the femoral artery can cause a casualty to bleed out internally quite rapidly. Finally the finger bones were found in a flexed position. Some of those who saw the remains interpreted this as evidence of the final agonies of the individual, with his fingers clenched in pain, but this flexing could have resulted from a variety of causes. Also, the skull damage, if relevant, would have been instantaneously fatal.

In terms of equipment, the soldier was quite lightly laden. Unlike German leather equipment, British 1908 webbing equipment was made, as its name implies, from canvas webbing. This rarely survives, although it was also made up of a mass of brass buckles, sliders and strap-ends which do generally survive well. The brass parts found suggest that no ammunition pouches or belt were present, and that the individual had only a 'PH Hood' gas mask in its bag, along with a few other items pushed into the gas hood bag and in his pockets. The gas hood bag would normally be worn across the shoulder to rest on the hip. In this case it was found just behind the left shoulder, a position it could easily have slipped to as the man fell. In addition to the gas hood itself, several candles were also found in the bag. A toothbrush and a set of anti-gas goggles were found in positions consistent with the tunic pockets, and in the area of the trouser pockets were discovered a standard issue jack-knife, and a leather purse of small change.

The most significant objects as far as this man's identity was concerned were a pair of brass regimental shoulder-titles *in situ* on either shoulder where they would have attached to the tunic shoulder straps. These read 'KINGS OWN' and refer to the King's Own (Royal Lancaster) Regiment. No documentary material was found, and there was no ID tag. In 1916 British practice was still to issue only one identity disc, which was removed at the time of death. Indeed, even had it not been removed, the 'vulcanised cardboard' from which they were made would have decayed after nearly ninety years in the soil.

So who was he and when did he die? The location of the body on top of the upcast spoil from the mine meant that he must have died on or shortly after 1 July 1916 (more than a year after the two Germans who lay nearby). A study of the British order of battle showed that only the 1st Battalion of the Kings Own had served in that area, forming the third wave of the 4th Division's attack on 1 July 1916. The 4th Division was a mostly regular army division, and indeed had an initially successful day on 1 July. The whole of the 'Heidenkopf' was captured and the division pushed on towards the German second line. Sadly the failure of the 'Pals' of the 31st Division to the north at Serre village and of the 29th Division to the south meant that the gains could not be sustained and the 4th Division eventually had to retreat to its own trenches.

At the end of the fighting the 1st Battalion Kings Own had suffered 387 casualties, including 122 dead, of whom 91 officers and men have no known grave and are recorded on the memorial at Thiepval. It is likely that the remains found were of one of these casualties, many of whom had to be abandoned in the German position when the battalion retreated back to its own trenches. Beyond that it is difficult to say which of those men he might be. The absence of web equipment may suggest that he was a stretcher-bearer, but a number of these men are also missing and he lacks some of the items associated specifically with such men. Equally his equipment may have been removed, either as he was being tended for his leg injury, or after his death. A British screw picket was found adjacent to his body. This may be coincidental, but might have been placed there as a marker, to indicate either a wounded or a dead man. Several speculative explanations are possible, but none is conclusive.

The case is not, however, closed quite yet. The purse of small change found in his trouser pocket contained a number of small denomination coins of both French and English types. Notable among them were several Jersey pennies, minted specially for use in the Channel Islands. The 1st Battalion Kings Own was among the troops who served as the Jersey garrison in the years leading up to the war, so it is possible that our soldier served there with the battalion. It is just possible that a cross-check of the names of those present on Jersey with those present on 1 July on the Somme will produce new information, but as yet the two relevant muster rolls have yet to be identified and examined.

Thus it was not possible to put a name on the stone which marks this soldier's grave. However, as has been stressed at various points throughout this book, that does not diminish his importance, or the respect paid to him by the excavation team, by the CWGC who provided a plot for him in Serre Cemetery No. 2, less than 200m from where he was found, or by the Kings Own Royal Border Regiment, now the Duke of Lancaster's Regiment (Kings, Lancashire and Border) who provided a funeral with full military honours in 2005.

This book opened with a description of that funeral, and the subsequent visitors to his grave. It closes with an acknowledgement of the debt of remembrance owed to him, and to millions like him from across the world. Men of all nations, those who died and those who lived, those who were wounded and those who survived unscathed: the soldiers of the Great War.

At the going down of the Sun, and in the morning,
we will remember them.[18]

Notes

1. M. Adkin, *The Waterloo Companion* (London, Aurum Press, 2001), p. 39.

2. J. Terraine, *The Smoke and the Fire, Myths and Anti-myths of War 1861–1945* (London, Sidgwick & Jackson, 1980), p. 51.

3. W. Tute, *The North African War* (London, Sidgwick & Jackson, 1976), p. 162.

4. M. Parker, *Monte Cassino* (London, Headline, 2003), p. 9.

5. Readers interested in this are directed to any of several works produced specifically on this subject, for example Dr Nicholas Saunders' recent book, *Trench Art: A Brief History and Guide, 1914–1939* (London, Leo Cooper/Pen and Sword Books, 2003).

6. HMSO, *Field Service Pocket Book* (1914; reprinted Newton Abbot, David & Charles, 1971), p. 88.

7. Letter by Wilhelm (surname unknown), a Kriegsfreiwilliger in the 2nd Battalion 215 Reserve Regiment, written on 18 October 1914. Private collection.

8. J.R. Innes, *Flash-spotters and Sound Rangers* (reprinted London, George Allen & Unwin, 1997), pp. 163–5.

9. R.A. Lloyd, *A Trooper in the Tins* (1938; reprinted in paperback by Leonaur), p. 240.

10. A. Clayton, *Paths of Glory: The French Army 1914–18* (London, Cassell, 2005).

11. P.G. Bales, *The History of the 1/4th Battalion Duke of Wellington's Regiment 1914–1919* (Naval & Military Press, 1920), p. 79.

12. D. Hibbert, *Wilfred Owen – A New Biography* (Weidenfeld & Nicolson, 2002).

13. G. Corrigan, *Sepoys in the Trenches* (Spellmount, 1999).

14. A. Rawson, *British Army Handbook 1914–18* (Stroud, Sutton, 2006).

15. T.J. Mitchell and G.M. Smith, *Official History of the War, Medical Services, Casualties and Medical Statistics* (London, HMSO, 1922).

16. T.B. Nicholls, *Organization, Strategy and Tactics of the Army Medical Services in War* (Bailliere, Tindall & Cox, 1936).

17. Hibbert, *Wilfred Owen*, p. 240.

18. Laurence Binyon, 'For the Fallen'.

INDEX